T0360593

Digital Transformation of the Supply Chain
A Practical Guide for Executives

Digital Transformation
of the Supply Chain
A Practical Guide for Executives

Albert Tan
SJTU Asia-Pacific Graduate Institute, Singapore

Sameer Shukkla

World Scientific

NEW JERSEY · LONDON · SINGAPORE · BEIJING · SHANGHAI · HONG KONG · TAIPEI · CHENNAI · TOKYO

Published by

World Scientific Publishing Co. Pte. Ltd.

5 Toh Tuck Link, Singapore 596224

USA office: 27 Warren Street, Suite 401-402, Hackensack, NJ 07601

UK office: 57 Shelton Street, Covent Garden, London WC2H 9HE

Library of Congress Cataloging-in-Publication Data
Names: Tan, Albert Wee Kwan, 1962– author. | Shukkla, Sameer, author.
Title: Digital transformation of the supply chain : a practical guide for executives /
  Albert Tan, Sameer Shukkla.
Description: Hackensack, NJ : World Scientific Publishing Co., [2021] |
  Includes bibliographical references and index.
Identifiers: LCCN 2021015355 | ISBN 9789811229596 (hardcover) |
  ISBN 9789811229602 (ebook) | ISBN 9789811229619 (ebook other)
Subjects: LCSH: Business logistics. | Executives.
Classification: LCC HD38.5 .T35 2021 | DDC 658.7--dc23
LC record available at https://lccn.loc.gov/2021015355

British Library Cataloguing-in-Publication Data
A catalogue record for this book is available from the British Library.

For any available supplementary material, please visit
https://www.worldscientific.com/worldscibooks/10.1142/12079#t=suppl

Desk Editor: Lai Ann

Typeset by Stallion Press
Email: enquiries@stallionpress.com

Printed in Singapore

This book unravels the complexities of supply chain process transformation by explaining step by step, and in simple terms, what are the requirements for success right from the basics to how to implement this complicated task. The book provides insights into how to lead the transformation project and how to manage the change internally and externally. The authors' hands-on experience in the field via applied research is clearly illustrated in the case studies which provide the reader with practical examples of the challenges and benefits of implementing a supply chain transformation project. A must-have book for all supply chain professionals.

Professor Cedwyn Fernandes
Pro-Vice Chancellor, Middlesex University, Dubai

Supply chain process transformation has become an essential part of competition in the global economy. This book provides an insightful approach on this re-engineering process based on solid research and practical examples. We have learned and applied some of the concepts to streamline our processes.

Mr. Teh Wee Chye
Managing Director, Malayan Flour Mills Bhd, Malaysia

Successful companies deliver the right product to the right customer at the right time and at the right price. This book provides a concise and clear explanation on the art of transformation towards enabling a Digital Supply chain. It challenges you on the old ways of doing thing in the supply chain and helps you to transform your supply chain for profitability and sustainability.

Mr. Hsiao Chink Tang
Senior Economist, East Asia Department, Asian Development Bank,
Philippines

Supply chain management in a company should no longer be relegated to a select group of people sitting in a logistics department. It is a cross-functional issue. Much like how companies nowadays thrust sales responsibilities to every employee, every division plays a key role in a supply chain process, like links in a complex chain of behaviours. The challenge is to change the mindset or culture of a company's employees from a silo, 'us versus them' mentality, to one of true team work. This book is an essential 'How To' guide to supply chain process transformation and should be seen as the guide to any company wanting to stay ahead of the competition.

Mr. Raymond Yee
Vice President of Customs & Regulatory Affairs, DHL Express
Singapore Pte Ltd, Singapore

PROLOGUE

Through the last few decades, latest technologies have improved processes within the four walls of a business, e-commerce has helped bridge communications between businesses and suppliers, and other supply chain systems are moving products to the market faster and more efficiently than ever. But the evolution hasn't stopped there. Today, supply chain digitalization is ushering in a whole new business model, one where real-time connectivity, greater visibility, real-time responsiveness, and anticipation will become the underlying characteristics of our businesses. But it won't happen overnight. It's up to businesses to build upon the incremental advancements offered by past solutions while working towards a networked, digitally connected future.

Companies, and by extension their supply chains, need to embark on a path down the digital road. It's not a simple or straightforward journey. Nor is it the same for every business. But it's a journey worth taking — not only for the sake of an end goal, but for all the benefits that come along the way. And while there's no single path to success, there are several shared traits among the leaders, no matter which industry they represent. From these examples, we begin to see specific digital building blocks, either technologies or processes, that comprise the foundation of a successful digital transformation. This book is an attempt to bring together new insights into how to lead a digital supply chain transformation project and how to manage the change internally and externally.

CONTENTS

Chapter 1

RELEVANCE OF DIGITAL TRANSFORMATION FOR SUPPLY CHAINS

We are undergoing the next great industrial revolution and judging by the speed at which we've seen digital disruption tear through industries, today's technology may be more disruptive than the revolutions driven by steam power, assembly lines, and the first computers. The rise of digital, data-driven technology has transformed entire industries, helping the smallest start-ups quickly establish a presence, scale in record time, and pave the way for entirely new business models. On the other hand, established brands that have turned a blind eye to the digital age, too satisfied with the status quo to change, are being toppled at alarming rates. While new technologies and digital solutions have slowly been introduced to different areas of business, many of those designed for supply chain have focused on solving well-known problems.

Today, all industry supply chains are at a cusp of innovation. 2020 has been a watershed year in terms of supply chain strategies across all industries without exception. Majority of companies across industries had some supply chain strategies pre-COVID-19 and quite a few digital supply chain initiatives in different stages of planning or execution. In the post-COVID-19 world, all these strategies are already being reconsidered. Supply chain visibility needs to take another step forward using real-time data integration across end-to-end entities and partners to enable more effective decision-making and boost cash flow benefits, measured by

1

working capital improvements. Truly, disruption is turning out to be the mother of innovation. So how to be the innovative supply chain and stay ahead to generate those cash flow benefits?

Adopting a digitally enabled transformation strategy will allow supply chains to take advantage of the upsides and maintain an agile and flexible cost base. Leading analysts and top Fortune 100 companies are already talking of digitally enabled themes that could be transforming supply chains in the near-term and medium-term future. So first we talk about what is the current situation and what supply chains can do today to be "rightly" prepared for disruptions, which are now understood as frequent norms. Supply chains need to realign their objectives in the face of:

- Changing population demographics based on increasingly urbanized population and new migrations that will happen once economic activity revives
- Constant pressure yet again to reduce costs and increase access to information across not just direct supply chain partners but across the ecosystem of partners
- Increased customer awareness with online information availability and real-time response expectations
- Renewed focus on resilience in supply chains, which is naturally linked to improving visibility across multi-tiers of supply chain partners
- Government reform programs and regulations influencing or dictating most industries.

Today, companies need to prepare supply chains for tomorrow's necessary digitalization by establishing the right foundation of processes. The 2020 situation, with the COVID-19 pandemic, highlighted the fact that levels of automation and digitalization are varying from above medium to quite low across industries such as pharmaceutical, retail, consumer goods, automotive, general manufacturing, oil and gas, and construction. Despite the supply and demand crisis which most companies have been put into, it makes for a good time to actively experiment and start on a path of agile and continuous improvement.

With customer centricity as a renewed focus of business strategy, the current global situation demands that companies across industries innovate and make their supply chains more agile and flexible. This need is also required to support key business tenets for improvements in efficiency, sustainability, customer centricity and reduction in material or resource waste. To achieve this, companies must focus on and tackle key business problems and current vulnerabilities like:

- Lack of visibility into the complex globally dispersed supply chain beyond direct suppliers
- Inability to accurately track the level of current and incoming material or finished product inventories to be sold
- No information on demand fluctuations, which will now vary with huge spikes and valleys
- Too much reliance on the workforce for more manual and time-intensive activities like data gathering and reporting
- Longer lead times and dependency on partners for production or supply of critical materials

In effect, 2020 has reinforced the need for businesses to embark on digital transformations of supply chains. It is also worthwhile to consider industry-specific imperatives. Let us take the example of the oil and gas industry. Decline in oil prices spells a supply chain optimization opportunity for the industry. With worldwide production outpacing demand, oil prices have fallen precipitously in recent years. Led by "lockdowns" where stay-at-home orders were imposed globally in efforts to curb the spread of COVID-19, the downturn in oil demand has been a moment of reckoning for the oil and gas industry. And on the other side, the demand will start increasing as people prefer personal to public transport in a post-pandemic world in a bid to reduce contact with others. The ability of the oil and gas industry to address a number of operational challenges will be critical in ensuring that future demand is met with adequate supply.

In the context of the oil industry, important precursors to a digital transformation will therefore look like this:

- Supply chain operating model design, i.e. a quick assessment of the existing situation and design and definition of the future state of digital operations

- Redefining the sales and operations planning process across organizational functions covering process, technology, software applications, roles and responsibilities, skill sets, reporting, key performance indicators (KPIs), and governance
- Software system enablement comprising of digital technology implementation, systems integration, useful business analytics, and relevant automation

Every industry presents unique supply chain challenges, and the oil and gas sector has its own share of complexity. Transporting products requires special equipment, working under very strict regulatory compliances, and need extensive safety procedures. Very often, oil and gas operations are carried out at remote locations, and run 24 hours, 7 days a week, for 365 days a year.

Supply chain management in the oil and gas industry often involves multiple modes and multiple tasks such as supplying materials for oil rigs to moving extremely heavy equipment and hazardous materials. At another level, we are talking about the hydrocarbon value chain. At one end, we have petroleum and petrochemical sources, and at the consumer end, we have gasoline and liquified petroleum gas. Along this path, there are multitudes of hydrocarbon products as direct products, by-products, and many chemical reagents, catalysts, and solvents. Oil and gas industry leaders have been working on following supply chain improvement levers:

- Rationalization of very complex supply chain networks to improve visibility and integration of the supply chain across different organizations in the hydrocarbon value chain. There will be many buyer–supplier relationships across these networks which demand simplification. We are now seeing companies even choosing to represent the supply chain network "radially" connected across partners — a massive shift from the linear representations of the past.
- Implementation of global cross-industry standards in processes, digital technologies, and people practices referencing oil and gas, chemical, and consumer industry characteristics to enable central source of mission critical data and associated ability to rapidly respond to real

world scenarios, such as a worldwide panic which can very quickly turn the demand and supply situation upside down.

- Improvements in real time information visibility, which in turn would provide the right foundation for any ability to perform "what if" simulation scenarios in the realm of supply chain planning to quickly adjust operating plans without throwing the core operational or production teams into a state of confusion.

- Digital collaboration across maximum supply chain partners to achieve the twofold objectives of making the supply chain initiative a mutually beneficial agenda and, with better information sharing, to improve basic efficiency of goods movement across the network.

We considered the oil and gas industry as an example above so that all possible industry supply chain characteristics are taken into consideration by a company while preparing for digital supply chain transformation. It may be interesting to note that, with some variations, the above recommendations will apply across all goods and services industries.

Retailers are finally acknowledging the customer as the center of their universe rather than the store. Following the lead of disruptive innovators like Amazon and Alibaba, and established giants like Walmart, retailers are evolving to give consumers the products they want, when they want them, wherever they may be. Meanwhile, in the consumer products industry, major players like Unilever and Procter & Gamble are blurring the lines between retail and online business models through new subscription services or Amazon Dash. Fashion and apparel brands such as Zara and H&M are investing in speed-enhancing the supply chain to drastically shorten the time it takes to go from concept to consumer. And automotive and industrial companies are working to reduce friction in the supply chain and enhance collaboration among suppliers. Businesses everywhere are starting to recognize the value of supply chain visibility, tying digital information to the real world, and turning insights into action.

As digital transformation progresses through supply chains, it becomes clear that certain supply chains are more mature than others. But none have achieved full digital maturity according to analyst reports globally. The digital journey takes companies, and by extension their supply chains, through a series of ordered stages. Each stage contains specific competencies and technologies necessary to build a platform for continued digital evolution.

Change is incremental. But as businesses gain proficiency within each stage, their supply chains become better-equipped to meet the demands of today's complex, networked, and global business environment. And while certain steps may seem small, it adds up to some truly transformative opportunities throughout the supply chain. For example, shipping companies must track their containers in real time, which have long been tracked using manual processes. Manual tracking is no longer acceptable and must be digitally transformed in order to be competitive. According to a futuristic technology vision report published by a leading management consulting firm in 2019, 45% of companies surveyed responded that the pace of innovation in their organizations had significantly accelerated over the preceding three years due to emerging digital technologies.

Chapter 2

IDENTIFYING PROCESSES FOR THE DIGITAL TRANSFORMATION OF THE SUPPLY CHAIN

In the 1990s, many companies adopted business process re-engineering to obliterate functional silos and create cross-functional, integrated, and process-based organizations. Despite multiple rounds of such attempts at process transformation, many supply chains are still not operating at the level of interconnections and collaborations that most industry leaders are adopting. Today, supply chain managers at the average performing company in any industry confront a new challenge of eliminating process disconnects and making yet another attempt to synchronize across process silos to unlock value. And COVID-19 exposed these shortcomings in supply chains to the world. Add to it the supply chain crisis across industries, unleashed by a 1,300 feet long container ship blocking the Suez Canal in 2021.

Digital supply chain transformation is a recommended approach to enable mutual adjustment of processes across different business functions or stakeholder groups to align key information, material, and cash flows across business processes to maximize returns and minimize losses. As we propound digital supply chain transformation in this chapter, we will focus on supply chain processes and transformation opportunities that companies need to imbibe as soon as they can. It is not harsh to say that survival for some will be based on these immediate actions. Oftentimes, failures of improvement across five key business functions can be costly and limit the true potential of organizations. Connecting across the supply chain, product development, distribution and sales, customer service and delivery, and financial functions to ensure that the right product is delivered to the right customer at the right time and at the right margin remains a challenge. Failures to synchronize across these core business functions can create direct losses or, even worse, eliminate opportunities to realize new growth. In contrast, companies that are already collaborating internally across functions are ready to collaborate externally as well with supply chain partners and thus outperform their competition with strategies that are seemingly difficult to imitate and execute.

Adopting key tenets of our recommended digital supply chain transformation has the potential for companies to radically change the work environment. Individual processes of disparate functions are combined to gain effectiveness, efficiency, and productivity. Shop floor workers are empowered and allowed to make decisions on the spot to eliminate process roadblocks or multiple hierarchy of approvals and increase speed to market. Not only is this beneficial for overall supply chain performance but it can also increase employee satisfaction and loyalty.

As we go beyond the COVID-19 pandemic, supply chains around the world will evolve to be completely different. In subsequent chapters, we talk about supply chain process transformation in a more general way so that readers are able to appreciate this beyond 2021. The real value of any supply chain transformation lies in the positive impact to people in an organization. Companies should consider digital supply chain transformation as fully successful when employees can expand their skill and knowledge into other areas and have the ability to make decisions that affect supply chain performance.

A few words on what digital supply chain transformation is NOT. It is not about reorganizing, restructuring, downsizing, automation, or cost cutting. All of these things may be a result of a well-thought-out, well-planned, and well-executed business process improvement project. However, the company's listed goals, mission, and vision should not be the sole reason for a company to justify a business transformation program. Of course, these are guiding principles.

In our experience, business transformations are typically carried out as complex, time-sensitive, large-scale, multi-million-dollar projects focused on designing and implementing fundamentally restructured supply chain processes. Improvement involves information management, technology, and people at every organization level and in a variety of functions, including engineering, manufacturing, supply chain, sales, product management, finance, human resources, information technology, and marketing.

A supply chain maturity model was proposed by Archie Lockamy and Kevin McCormack in 2004 to determine how integrated a company's supply chain is, as shown in Figure 1. The model conceptualizes how process maturity relates to the Supply Chain Operations Reference (SCOR) model framework, which was developed by the Supply Chain Council, an independent non-profit organization considered as a benchmark and standards defining entity for supply chain management. It was designed for effective communication among supply chain partners and can be used to describe, measure, and evaluate supply chain configurations. The current version of the model is owned by the Association for Supply Chain Management. As we know, SCOR is based on five distinct management processes: plan, source, make, deliver, and return.

The model consists of five maturity levels:

Level 1 — Ad hoc: The supply chain and its practices are unstructured and ill-defined. Processes, activities, and organizational structures are not based on horizontal processes, while process performance is unpredictable.

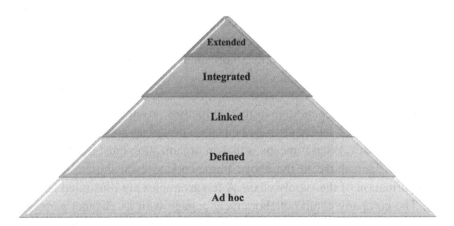

Figure 1. Maturity model for supply chain process integration (Lockamy & McCormack, 2004)

Supply chain management costs are high, customer satisfaction is low, and cross-functional cooperation is also low.

Level 2 — Defined: Basic supply chain processes are defined and documented, but the activities and organization basically remain traditional. Supply chain management costs remain high and customer satisfaction has improved but is still low. Representatives from functions meet regularly to coordinate with one another concerning process activities, but only as representatives of their traditional functions.

Level 3 — Linked: This level represents the breakthrough. Cooperation between intra-company departments, suppliers, and customers is established. Cross-functional and cross-company teams that share common process measures and goals are formed. Supply chain costs begin decreasing, and customer satisfaction begins to show a marked improvement.

Level 4 — Integrated: The company, its customers, and suppliers cooperate on the process level. Organizational structures are based on supply chain management procedures; supply chain management performance measures and management systems are applied. Advanced supply chain management practices such as collaborative forecasting with other members of a supply chain are formed. Consequently, supply chain costs are markedly reduced.

Level 5 — Extended: Competition is based on supply chains or "multi-firm networks". Collaboration between companies is on the highest level — multi-firm supply chain management teams with common processes, goals, and broad authority form a horizontal working group. Customer-focused, collaborative culture is in place.

Digital supply chain transformation focuses on supply chain maturity level 4 and level 5 where cross-organization processes are fundamental to their businesses. What it means is that an organization must be at a maturity level 3 or above in the above framework to even initiate a digital transformation of the supply chain. A few examples are illustrated here:

The company could collaboratively engage with its channel partners or resellers in joint demand forecasting and sales planning. A step further, another company could involve suppliers in collaborative product design and engineering. Another company would undertake the path of a refreshed inventory optimization and distribution channel management initiative to redefine parameters and policies. Yet another initiative for an organization would be to review and redesign the global supply chain network and carry out renewed financial planning. Another company would simply want to refresh the human talent for digital supply chain transformation through human resources acquisition, deployment, and optimization.

The maturity level tells us one criterion by which a company should consider defining the process scope of a particular digital supply chain transformation initiative. However, that is more of an inward-looking assessment of what processes we can pick up based on where we are currently. In our view, we also need to juxtapose this with external market trends or industry peer group initiatives. This helps the candidate company ensure that they are ready from a pre-requisites standpoint to embark on the digital supply chain transformation journey, and at the same time identify a scope of processes for digital transformation based on relevant industry initiatives. This kind of overlaying helps us to also make sure that the scope of processes for supply chain transformation is relevant to the needs of our customers and therefore high in relevance. We notice some digital initiatives that have seen the most traction in recent years and are being implemented by quite a few companies across industries.

Quite a few companies are establishing relevance for smart contracts using blockchain to better identify suppliers and negotiate better prices and service levels. Others are carrying out advanced predictive spend analysis to redefine procurement and sourcing strategies. Most manufacturing organizations are defining criteria and parameters for a procurement visibility control tower. Some of them are going a few steps back to first identify scenarios and business processes for exception handling through advanced analytics powered by machine learning and artificial intelligence. We are also aware of many companies moving towards automated requisition to purchase order creation and release to supplier, learning the buyer's routine activities through robotic process automation (RPA). Companies are also reviewing and enhancing purchasing processes in their enterprise resource planning (where available) to enable automated reminders to suppliers on non-receipt of acknowledgment or advanced shipping notice as expected. Many companies are now implementing automated goods receipt processing and invoice reconciliation leveraging optical character recognition. With advanced maturity in sourcing processes established, organizations are also moving towards consolidation of purchase requirement quantities from different sources to align to minimum order quantity of suppliers.

Even prior to the COVID-19 pandemic and its effects on the demand for goods and services, the economic situation in many countries had already prompted companies to implement segmented demand and supply planning for maintaining optimum inventory. Many of them also started to improve their supply chain monitoring by sales and operations planning dashboard creation and publishing by roles. Consensus demand planning workflow activities are now being established by those companies that have already matured on the consensus process. And some are going the next step of implementing demand sensing by incorporating external factors into demand plan leveraging artificial intelligence/machine learning algorithms. Quite a few organizations are now collaborating in real-time with channel partners or resellers in joint demand forecasting and sales planning, leveraging a cloud-based supply chain collaboration platform.

In the outbound logistics realm, almost all leading companies in every industry are beginning to convert transport plans and schedules to meaningful summary dashboards summarizing KPIs such as full truck load and on-time delivery using advanced analytics. There are also recent initiatives to enable real-time tracking of handling equipment and other devices within warehouses and distribution centers, leveraging on the Internet of things. Many organizations are now utilizing on robotic process automation to support the searching of materials and other services for warehouse operations, while at the physical level, most companies are implementing robotic picking, packing, sorting, and loading of shipments in warehouses.

While establishing the roadmap for supply chain transformation, it is important to keep in mind the goals that need to be realized over time, as shown in Figure 2. Setting quantifiable goals is the first necessary step, and based on the stated goal and desired outcome, the company should further investigate the exact scope of change — what process must undergo the transformation. Finally, it is worth simulating how the

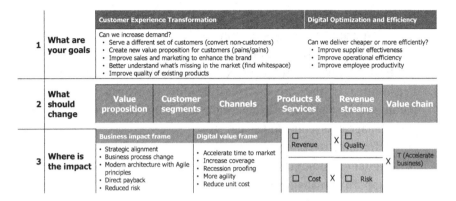

Figure 2. Aligning goals with business impacts

proposed change will impact the business and compare the risks versus rewards of pursuing it.

In a supply chain transformation project, there will be a number of processes that can be considered for redesign and upliftment towards digitalization. It is therefore important to select a few of these processes from the long list due to resource constraints. The starting point in selecting a process for improvement is to obtain information from stakeholders about their satisfaction or dissatisfaction and key business pain points with the specific supply chain processes and sub-processes that they are handling. Key criteria to consider in the process selection include:

1. Importance: does the process have strategic relevance? Does it support corporate strategy and any of the overall critical success factors for the business? Does it have significant positive impact on the company's customers or the performance of suppliers and channel partners? At its core, does this process potentially improve business performance on a periodic basis?

2. Performance: does the process have the following performance deficiencies?
   • Repeated or frequent internal and external customer complaints
   • Extensive information exchange
   • Data redundancies across sub-processes within the process
   • Excessive hand-offs within this process or with either processes

- Long queuing time
- Redundant checking and control
- Frequent rework and iteration
- Extra complexity, frequent exceptions, and special handling needs
3. Feasibility: is the process feasible for transformative change? Parameters by which we can determine feasibility include the following:
   - Manageable scope and scale
   - Affordable to change
   - Digital technologies readily available
   - Supportive management
   - Acceptable culturally
   - Viable politically
4. Potential for new digital technology: can new technology dimensions, such as the below, be introduced to improve the process?
   - Cloud-based shared databases and blockchain
   - Latest-generation telecommunication networks powering Internet of things (IoT)
   - Advanced decision support tools powered by artificial intelligence or machine learning
   - Wireless data communication and portable computing devices as small as mobile phones
   - Automatic identification and tracking technology including high-tech sensors
   - Geographical information systems powered by real-time connected Global Positioning System

Based on past experience, the scope of the digital transformation program for the supply chain should be based on an organization's capabilities, the different types of available resources, as well as the level of interest from suppliers, customers, or other partners. Even if given a clear need to transform, most organizations would lack sufficient resources, such as people, funds, and time, to do so. It is best to organize and start the overall digital supply chain transformation program with small projects for organizations that have not done any transformation before. Once people demonstrate that they can handle simple changes to processes, more complicated ones can be tackled subsequently. Thus, each successful initiative becomes a model for future efforts.

7-Eleven (www.7-eleven.com) in Japan has transformed its supply chain to quickly respond to sudden changes in demand instead of fast or cheap deliveries. By investing in proprietary real-time systems for visibility into customer demographics, preferences, and sales at every store, the company is able to identify new sales opportunities and alert suppliers to potential shifts in requirements, to reallocate inventory among stores, and ensure that the company restocks at the right time. Having strong partnerships with its suppliers and by using a variety of transportation modes, including trucks, motorcycles, boats, and even helicopters, the company is able to resupply and replenish stores three or more times a day. This allows the company to cater to different consumer segments and demands at different hours, from delivering bento boxes for lunch to other fresh food for breakfast and dinner.

Chapter 3

INITIATING THE DIGITAL TRANSFORMATION OF THE SUPPLY CHAIN

We recommend that companies must think about a digital transformation for their supply chain by starting with a comprehensive assessment of supply chain processes and the various skill sets required for key roles in the organization that would be required to drive this kind of initiative. The expected outcome is to recommend improvement opportunities and a roadmap for future investments based on extensive research that will improve operational efficiency and digital supply chain experience for individual supply chain functions, as well as stakeholders from other business functions who need supply chain information. Some examples of leading practices that are already being adopted to initiate a digital supply chain transformation by companies are as follows:

- Identify opportunities and levers to optimize "spend" via strategic sourcing and contract management
- Leverage subject matter experts at the supplier end. For the buying organization, this helps procurement managers and buyers to focus on value creation, rather than consuming time in mundane work.
- Engage internal "customers" in the decision-making process
- Identify levers for supply chain velocity improvement

- Carry out thorough assessment for fitment of advanced digital supply chain planning solutions available in the market with the best in-class automation and analytics capabilities
- Holistically re-engineer demand sensing and demand planning to incorporate aspects of all potential market dynamics and newer causes of variability
- Establish policy and procedures so that we can enable supplier-managed inventory
- Define and execute centralized inventory management processes for enterprise-wide visibility
- Constantly review inventory policy and parameters, leveraging a digital twin that can do this much more frequently

Companies looking to execute this kind of assessment as the right process foundation for a digital supply chain transformation must leverage a holistic framework approach, focusing on supply chain maturity assessment covering end to end supply chain planning, sourcing to contracting to operational procurement, collaboration with all supply chain partners, and end to end logistics comprising warehousing and transportation. This approach to supply chain performance assessment would run over three stages:

Stage 1: Supply chain process evaluation
Focused on evaluating existing processes, the integration of supply chain functions, roles, and responsibilities, and alignment with strategic goals.
Stage 2: Exploring emerging technology for breakthrough performance
Focused on evaluating the usage of existing applications' capabilities and what best can be done by enhancing them to meet the desired outcomes.
Stage 3: Digital transformation of the supply chain
Focused on assessing the various technologies and applications that currently exist and are planned in the digital strategy roadmap, and what further actions need to be taken to become among the leaders in the industry for supply chain excellence.

While establishing the roadmap for supply chain transformation, it is important to keep in mind that outcomes need to be realized over time, where

- "Quick wins" are a set of initiatives that can be done with minimum investment of time and cost to get quick returns (~ McCormack Maturity Level 3 or 4)
- "Tactical gains" can be achieved by initiatives for a mid-term range, which will improve core supply chain process capabilities to a good extent (~ McCormack Maturity Level 4)
- "Strategic success" will be realized by initiatives that strive to significantly improve supply chain performance in a way that it positively impacts the long-term goals of the organization (~ McCormack Maturity Level 5)

A clear business case about the need for change and where the change is going to take us is necessary for successfully selling digital supply chain transformation to each of the supply chain partners (e.g. suppliers, customers, logistics providers, and so on). The key purpose of this stage is to mobilize project resources and establish a common understanding of program scope, activities, milestones, and accountabilities.

Five fundamental steps are required in the creation of a digital supply chain transformation program to ensure that the supply chain program is successful.

1. Establishing the core team: identify and announce the business owner of the supply chain transformation program. The business owner will then nominate the program manager and one supply chain process SME to start the preparation activities.
2. Mutual goal setting: establish targets for the organization and its supply chain partners. Identify program participants from within and partner organizations. Confirm the roles and responsibilities for all stakeholders and develop program governance structure. Emphasize that the fundamental goal of an integrated supply chain is the desire to improve operating efficiency or to manage cost more effectively than competitors. Have a cross-functional and cross-partners workshop

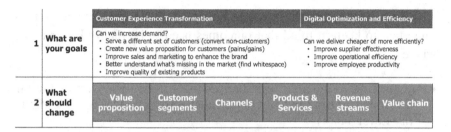

Figure 3. Goal setting

to answer one thematic question: how will this process improve the supply chain performance? A sample goal setting schematic is shown here in Figure 3.

3. Business model canvas: identify and assess stakeholders who can potentially affect the program using the business model canvas (created by Alexander Osterwalder, co-founder of Strategyzer). The business model canvas is a useful tool to help you understand a business model in a straightforward, structured way. Using this canvas will lead to insights about the customers you serve, what value propositions are offered through various channels, and how your company makes money. You can also use the business model canvas to determine the key processes and technologies that can transform the business (the authors' client made use of the business model canvas to map their current business, as seen in Appendix 1, and future businesses, as illustrated in Appendix 2).

The business model canvas can be extended to finalize program scope, objectives, and timing in the context of the company supply chain's strengths and weaknesses. Assess the external threats and opportunities in the supply chain to create a logical framework for comparing the strengths and weaknesses of the various alternative sources of supply and demand. What are the external threats and opportunities in developing the supply chain?

4. Coordination and planning across supply chain partners: create and maintain relationships in order to develop long-term trust and support. Planning has two levels: buyer–supplier coordination and production–distribution coordination.

Level 1: Buyer–supplier coordination — attain steady supply of raw materials and resources for the project.

Level 2: Product-distribution coordination — link development to product transfer to the customer. How can the firm optimally structure the supply chain to ensure cost and resource flow efficiently?

The core team needs to conduct a series of program kick-off meetings to engage stakeholders, align expectations, and gather support for the program within its own organization and with participating supply chain partners. This is also the stage to create and socialize the overall program plan across all stakeholders in terms of the responsibilities of the key people and milestones to be achieved by accomplishing tasks over a feasible timeline.

5. Establish governance and control mechanism: identify and agree on ways to measure performance for all business processes in the scope of the digital supply chain transformation and adjust the flow of resources or mix of suppliers as needed. How can the company be sure that it is getting maximum performance (for example, highest efficiency in a process as applicable) from its supply chain? How can the company improve it?

Historical data as a representation of the anomalies and outliers in supply chain processes is of paramount importance in establishing the improvement opportunities based on true facts. Hence, an approach to the collection of historical data along with very clearly defined and agreed accountability for the same needs to be established right at the start. This is especially so in the context of digital transformation, where most digital evangelists the world over have said, it is all about "data, data, data".

The goal of most digital supply chain transformation programs is to create a coordinated supply chain planning and execution network that allows for optimal material acquisition, production, shipping, and distribution of goods and services among supply chain members. Digital supply chain transformation is not an easy process, nor should it be approached without sufficient understanding of the steps involved and the organization-wide commitment to a methodology that is required for it to work. Its benefits are obvious: integrated, logical supplier networks; clear links to customers; a streamlined flow of materials (raw, financial, and human) to the project planning; and significant expansion.

Traditionally, project planning often means simply scheduling, with a bit of risk analysis or work breakdown structure included sometimes. In digital supply chain transformation, it means that planning takes a whole new level of complexity. Planning begins outside of the project and the project organization; it begins with suppliers, customers, logistics providers, and others. It analyzes each of their potential contributions, selects those that will best benefit the project organization, and coordinates their deliveries. Hence, the new project planning is no longer an internal process simply involved in project development; it is a totally coordinated exercise with explicit links to the rest of the organization, suppliers, and customers. As an important prerequisite, a complete list of deliverables and program governance mechanisms should be jointly agreed upon by all supply chain and other cross-functional stakeholders at this stage of initiating the digital transformation program. When properly established and continually monitored and upgraded, digital supply chain transformation offers companies a new and powerful way of reconfiguring its supply chain. The initial time spent up-front establishing the supply chain will pay off for itself downstream as projects come to the market cheaper and with more direct customer feedback and acceptance. Below, we highlight the initial steps towards digital supply chain transformation recently undertaken by a construction services company in the Asia-Pacific region.

The company PQR is a multi-billion-dollar construction company headquartered in India. The organization expected the procurement function to be more proactive than reactive. The company's chief experience officer-level leadership expected to see the procurement function being involved in major decisions for the company. The organization started with structuring policies to eradicate procurement bypass wherein divisions used to ignore procurement suggestions and research in their day-to-day and planned requirements purchases. As such, they carried out a sourcing and procurement process assessment to identify potential areas wherein they could bring in digital levers such as artificial intelligence/machine learning (AI/ML), robotic process automation (RPA) and blockchain, and others as applicable. Some of the key business needs that were identified and placed on a digital supply chain transformation roadmap are listed below.

First, the company identified core business systems and solutions that were already being used by procurement functions: e-sourcing and e-auctions, electronic catalogs, contract management, supplier information management, e-procurement, e-invoicing, and spend analytics.

Using these as the foundation, the company started on what they called an "artificial intelligence discovery mission". The following levers were identified:

- Collaborative supplier networks leveraging a digital cloud-based platform
- Supplier risk management enabled by futuristic risk modeling based on internal and external parameters, leveraging predictive analytics
- Robotic Process Automation was identified to automate the operational procure-to-pay side of procurement. The processes herein are heavy in volume, highly transactional in nature, and need investment of both time and resources. Key benefits envisaged from RPA include minimizing human touchpoints, leading to enhanced purchase order management, and maintaining a strong audit trail for the future.

Once a person in charge of procurement makes a decision on the purchase, she expects RPA to trigger alerts to different departments of the organization, such as plant (to plan the output and resource utilization), marketing (plan for promotional activities), sales (to book orders based on the output and promotions), and finance (analysis of profit and loss, operating cost). With the above situation, the procurement process will be more strategic to the organization.

- Cognitive computing and AI: one of the major issues faced by buyers has been determining the cost factors in building a finished product. When a buyer does a strategic assessment of the raw materials, she needs to understand the price influencers of the material with the help of AI. When a buyer chooses a product and its United Nations Standard Products and Services Code, AI should be able to pull data regarding the availability of the dependent material, its historical pricing, current suppliers, global market availability, best possible location to procure from, quality standards, best available route for delivery, lead time to plant, and lead time to market.

- Predictive/advanced analytics via AI: for procurement of services from the market, the company expects that with the help of AI, buyers would be able to find out the skillset rates fixed by different labor boards, skilled workforce availability in the market, and current market rates.
- Intuitive user-friendly visualization tools

Thereafter, the digital innovation team identified emerging solutions and digital technologies that could impact sourcing and procurement in the future:

- Blockchain: the current situation with paper-based contracts have the following obvious and well-known problems:
  - Time consuming contract authoring, workflow, approvals, and documentation and signatures process
  - Inherent security risks
  - High administrative costs that keep increasing
  - Need for physical storage space

    Blockchain in procurement would be one of the initiatives for error-free and trustworthy business deals. No more invoice reconciliation, no more approval for payments, no more three-way match required for goods receipts.
- 3D printing
- Sensors/wearables
- Cyber tracking
- Virtual reality/spatial analytics

Chapter 4

ESTABLISHING ORGANIZATION AND PEOPLE READINESS

From a practical execution perspective, setting up the organization structure, ways of working, and a clear distribution of responsibilities and accountabilities should be a very integral part of initiating the digital supply chain transformation that we discussed in Chapter 3. At the same time, this topic is extremely important and critical to the expected success of a digital supply chain transformation program and therefore, it merits a complete chapter of its own.

The program would take shape based on the identification of scope from aspects we outlined in Chapter 2. Based on the process scope of supply chain management, there would be a program sponsor, already identified by the company leadership, representing the overall supply chain function for the company. This person would have identified one of the senior employees of the supply chain management function or department to lead this digital transformation program. This person can be called the program director, program manager, transformation leader, or transformation manager for the digital supply chain transformation program. Ultimately, it is the role, set of responsibilities, and deliverables that this person will be the single point of ownership for, that is important. We will come back to define this all-important role later. First of all, let us talk about how to structure the organization for such a critical business initiative: the digital supply chain transformation program that is bound to have both revenue and profitability impact on the company.

There are many structures that have been employed by different organizations in the past many years for any kind of business transformation, digital implementation, or similar programs. The traditional approach has been to establish a core team for the program, as shown in Appendix 3. This would typically involve representatives of the departments that have a stake in the program from a process standpoint. Also, there would be focused representatives from the information technology department for each process area in scope to bring in the digital application or digital technologies perspective into every stage of the program. This core program team would report to a steering committee or steering group. The steering group would comprise department heads and/or executive leadership team members of the company. The leading practice for supply chain transformation is to have the chief supply chain officer or equivalent as the head of this steering committee, and also the program sponsor. Depending on the strategic importance of the digital transformation program, the chief financial officer, chief information officer, and/or chief digital officer and chief executive officer would also be a part of the steering committee. The core team then enlists additional program or project members from other departments, from a consulting or digital services organization, digital application or technology provider, to partner organizations such as channel partners or suppliers depending on the scope of the supply chain process transformation being initiated. Thus, we are recommending the following approach and structure to setup the program organization for a digital supply chain transformation.

First, the program sponsor needs to set up the core team with a size of five to seven members, which seems to function most effectively. While a larger team size is not uncommon, studies have shown that core teams with more than 10 members may have trouble reaching consensus and achieving objectives. Key selection principles are as follows:

- Companies must identify a high-caliber, multidisciplinary core team which will bring a right mix of domain and technology expertise to deliver the digital supply chain assessment outcomes
- The core digital transformation team should collectively have many man-years of experience in supply chain process and business applications thought leadership

- Ideally, the core team's experience should pan across process and discrete industries or across manufacturing and retail scenarios. Essentially, we are talking about diverse experience types.
- The core team's focus should be on maximizing the positive impact of supply chain improvements to revenue growth and profitability improvements
- Considering that the digital supply chain transformation must bring about innovation and improve agility for the organization, it will be very useful to have one or two people with design thinking knowledge and an Agile certification as part of the core team

Second, the program sponsor needs to set up the steering committee, which includes himself and peers. As mentioned above, this would comprise the functional or department leaders and chief experience officers, as applicable to the strategic nature of the supply chain transformation program. The program sponsor needs to also have a formal meeting with these identified steering committee members and introduce the program director as the single point of contact to them.

Thirdly, an operating committee needs to be set up as an optional team driving towards program success. This is an optional part of the digital supply chain transformation program structure and is required to be instilled purely depending on the scope and timelines of the program. The operating committee should ideally include business process leads for the supply chain process areas in scope, the program director and digital technology leads from the information technology department, and the program manager or equivalent lead from the consulting or technology partner organization. As a general guide, two criteria for the need for an operating committee in the program structure are the overall program duration and number of supply chain process areas in scope. If the defined digital supply chain transformation scope is for end-to-end supply chain planning (demand planning, sales and operation planning, inventory planning and optimization, supply and procurement planning, production scheduling, distribution planning, transportation planning and optimization) and the program duration is at least six months, we definitely need an operating committee in place as a fortnightly progress review team, which is empowered to make tactical decisions for sustained progress.

The steering committee then reviews once every four to six weeks and provides strategic direction and decisions and conflict resolutions.

Next, we set up the overall project teams at the operational level. Traditionally, project teams operate at the periphery of the organization, pulling human, technical, and monetary resources away from the functional areas, suppliers, or customers for their own needs. In some cases, it has been seen that a digital transformation project being driven by the information technology or supply chain department will have team members assigned from other departments by managers choosing subordinates who are currently available. Those people are put on the digital transformation program regardless whether they possess the technical qualifications, people skills, or administrative abilities to perform effectively. In some examples, members have been assigned to supply chain transformation projects as a method for getting them out of their current departments, for some background reasons, and making them someone else's problem. We strongly recommend not to follow this thought process.

The choice of team members for the digital supply chain transformation program should be largely governed by the area of the core business process to be transformed. Since activities at any point in a process impact the activities throughout the process, project team members must be selected from all key points and interfaces throughout the process. This ensures that both knowledge of the total process and multiple perspectives are developed at different points along the way. As an example, when we talk about the order fulfillment process that is cross-functional in nature, the company's customers can also be involved as part of the team to provide vital perspectives in enhancing the new process design.

Now let us discuss in more details about the responsibilities and deliverables of the program director or equivalent, chosen by the program sponsor to lead the digital supply chain transformation program. At a minimum, he or she will have the following responsibilities:

- Reach a common understanding with the steering committee on the objectives and goals of the digital supply chain transformation program
- Schedule and lead a series of thoroughly prepared and well-structured program kick-off sessions

- Schedule and run core team meetings and steering committee and operating committee reviews
- Arrange for all types of resources, program budgeting, and funding
- Decide how much time the team will devote to the program
- Communicate with the steering committee and operating committee on the progress of the projects and any obstacles faced
- Launch data collection activities as part of program kick-off itself. (e.g. process models, information technology architecture diagrams, operational data)
- Schedule business interviews, working sessions, and review meetings with internal as well as external stakeholder groups
- Create and deliver the completed program plan with governance structure, milestones, dependencies, and resource loading
- Create and deliver data request templates to respective business and technology teams for data extraction from incumbent systems of record

A kick-off workshop should be carried out with the steering committee of the program or with the staff planning function to agree on the implementation schedule. During this workshop, each digital application and process needs to be assessed based on a variety of criterion. These criterion can be proposed by facilitators, but should be verified by business managers. It is important to identify and agree on the criteria before supply chain process assessment begins. Once a consensus on the priority of applications has been reached, facilitators, taking into consideration the business and policy developments, will need to drive the program plan.

Finally, setting up a structure and methods of interactions among all these groups within the program organization is of paramount importance and recommended as an integral step to setting up the program for success, even though this is not a group by itself. The core team should also establish a series of cadence meetings with the overall program team, the operating committee, the steering committee, and with the overall business community for the supply chain function.

Chapter 5

SUPPLY CHAIN PROCESS ASSESSMENT FOR DIGITAL TRANSFORMATION

The first step in process assessment for digital supply chain transformation is process mapping. Let us begin by defining "process" once again, in our context. A process is defined as a system of interdependent steps to deliver a desired output or service. Components of a process consist of:

- Process objective: specifies what is to be achieved by the process for the customer or organization
- Process owner: a person who has responsibility and authority for the running and management of the process
- Starting/ending activity within a process: key tasks or steps within a process that will consume time and utilizes some resources
- Inputs: information, goods, and services that are supplied for the process
- Outputs: goods and services produced by a process for the internal or external customers
- Process measurements: metrics in terms of cost, time, and quality as part of key performance indicators

Michael Hammer and James Champy (1993) offer the following definition of a business process: "A collection of activities that takes one or more kinds of input and creates an output that is of value to the customer".

A supply chain process is different from a function or a department. Some processes might be contained within a departmental function, while others cut across organizational boundaries to serve the customer. They operate horizontally through a company, in contrast to the vertical division of labor in traditional functional groupings. A supply chain process often involves multiple users and activities that take place at different timings. Not only do we need to examine the activities in which inputs are converted into outputs but we also need to be able to identify the correct sequence of activities. A common approach is to attempt some form of function decomposition, peeling the layers of the process onion, until one reaches the core components in that process.

Some organizations find it difficult to correctly determine their supply chain processes because they tend to think in terms of departments or functions, not in terms of the work they actually do, and the manner in which this work is performed. Cross-functional processes often go unmanaged because rarely is there an identified process owner — a person responsible for ensuring that the process is well-defined and capable of achieving its intended results.

One useful technique for naming processes is to identify their beginning and their end. For example, the order-fulfillment process could be called the "order to payment process". This will allow us to include steps that are not structurally housed in the sales department. Naming the processes in this way helps to break the structures, usually the functional paradigm, and to focus on the work of people. Processes can be classified into three types:

Management processes: these processes are meant for the organization to ensure that proper planning and management of long-term organization goals are developed and executed. Examples of management processes include setting vision/goals, product planning, marketing and sales, and supply chain management.

Primary or operational processes: these are the main supply chain processes that will provide value addition to the customers. There may be four to five primary processes, and examples include product line planning and management, product development, customer acquisition, demand and supply planning, sourcing and procurement, order fulfillment, logistics and transportation, customer servicing, licensing, etc.

Support or enabling processes: these supporting processes are required to enable primary processes to operate. Examples of such processes include human resource management, information technology development, facilities management, and corporate accounting.

A process map shows all the processes within the organization chart and encompasses the first level of processes that typically yield 5 to 10 core processes that define the business. The process map shown in Figure 4 is a high-level representation of the core processes for a telecom company. This map shows the core processes and their relationship to each other and the customer. It has only seven core supply chain processes, and it includes the customer as its focus.

At the next level, approximately 20 or more processes are identified. These are still at a relatively high level and have clear owners, usually comprising senior managers. The process details can be drawn using a flow chart or a swim-lane diagram (see Figure 5).

Supply chain processes traditionally cut across organizations and, consequently, suffer from a lack of coordination. Over time, this lack of coordination gives rise to practices that foster functional interests at the expense of process objectives, resulting in a loss of efficiency and customer focus. The key purpose of the process mapping phase is to review processes in order to refocus on customer needs and achieve quantum improvements in process efficiency at, possibly, reduced operating costs. Another key purpose of this phase is to get an understanding of the existing capabilities of processes for long-term, mid-term, and short-term planning and execution for the supply chain with a magnifier focus on sales and operations planning and sales and operations execution handoff. It is also important to understand existing roles and responsibilities of different supply chain functions, current system capabilities implemented, and further technological enablement planned in line with strategic directions by reviewing necessary documentation and artefacts. The next step is to identify opportunities for process improvement by means of conducting focused discussions and workshops across stakeholders for supply chain business processes and technology.

Each key supply chain process is mapped to understand how they interact with other supply chain partners and their relationship or dependency. The key processes are analyzed in detail so as to understand their

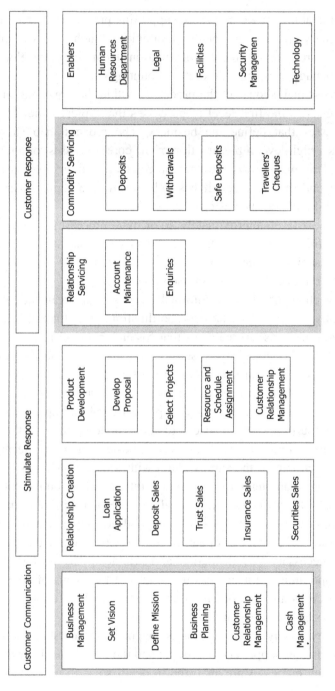

Figure 4. Core processes of a telecom company

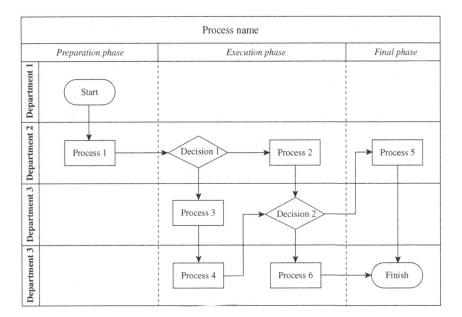

Figure 5.   Swim-lane representation of business processes

limitations and performance. Opportunities for improvement are identified. It would be very useful to leverage a formal supply chain process maturity model assessment questionnaire (for example, based on Lockamy and McCormack's framework) as a tool for process mapping.

The key activities to be performed to successfully accomplish process mapping are listed here:

1. Carry out evaluation of supply chain processes in terms of people or function owning the process steps
2. Review business strategy and planning documents, and current business and technology initiatives, and identify their implications to the supply chain
3. Read through the process flows, standard operating procedure documents, reporting and monitoring processes, manuals etc.
4. Prepare questionnaires for detailed stakeholder discussions/workshops
5. Read through the current strategy and process documentations, current technology platforms, information technology strategy roadmap with tools/technology, and implementation plans

6. Review documentation on various commercial off-the-shelf (COTS) applications for supply chain functions to understand their futuristic digital capabilities and how it can drive benefits for supply chain planning and collaboration with internal and external partners

Once we have completed the supply chain business process mapping, the next step is to carry out detailed process analysis. The key processes will need to be analyzed in detail in order to determine the performance gap, and opportunities for improvements will be identified. The following techniques are commonly used for process analysis.

Customer Analysis: Identification and Segmentation of Customers

Not all customers have the same needs. If these needs are sufficiently diverse, it may be necessary to segment the customer base according to differing needs and to analyze each segment separately. The implications of these differences would then have to be taken into account in process design to ensure that the needs of each segment are adequately catered for. Segmentation is the process of identifying groups of customers with enough common characteristics to enable the design of a product or service for each group's needs. Customer needs may differ in terms of:

- Emphasis, inclusion, or exclusion of different elements of the service/product provided by the organization
- Requirements or preferences in different elements or features of the service/product provided by the organization (which give rise to differences in difficulty or complexity in providing these elements)
- Degree of flexibility, responsiveness, or customization required
- Minimum quality or standards of the product/service that the customer is willing to accept (and hence the price that the customer is willing to pay for it)
- The urgency with which the customer views the completion of the service or delivery of the product. This would be measured in terms of the lead time that the customer is able to agree to for the selling company to commit to for delivering the service or product

- The quantity of the product demanded or volume of work generated by the customer's needs
- The location at which the service is to be performed or delivery of products is to be made

These differences may give rise to the need for:

- Staff with different levels of skill or knowledge to handle different customer groups
- The speed with which certain tasks need to be undertaken or priority/ attention given
- The familiarity of staff with specific customers and their needs and the amount of initiative required of staff
- The ability to handle variable workloads, and hence perform load balancing and resource scheduling (e.g. some segments might provide a steady stream of work, while others might be "lumpy" or show seasonality)
- Performing certain tasks or taking certain measures for some customer groups (and not others)
- Selecting different quality versus productivity or cost trade-off combinations for different customer segments.

The contribution of each segment to total profitability (or other appropriate measures of gain to the organization or its mission) should be determined. This should guide the amount of resources to be committed in serving each customer segment.

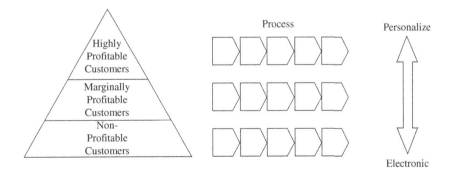

Figure 6.   Customize process for each customer segment

Segmentation may eventually imply exceptional tasks or specialized staff to handle certain customer segments or a process with multiple channels at some points. In the extreme case, completely separate (duplicated) process streams may need to be established to handle each segment. By referring to Figure 6, we can offer personalized services to highly profitable customers, while we can advise non-profitable customers to use online banking to reduce the cost to serve them. The marginally profitable customers can still make use of the automated teller machine or the bank teller, which provide some form of assistance for them.

Standardization promotes productivity and cost efficiency. Having differences in customer segments tends to work against standardization, and hence productivity and cost efficiency. This will have to be weighed against the gains expected in better satisfying the needs of each customer group.

A performance evaluation matrix is a convenient tool to evaluate the importance of each customer's needs versus the performance of the current process, as shown in Figure 7.

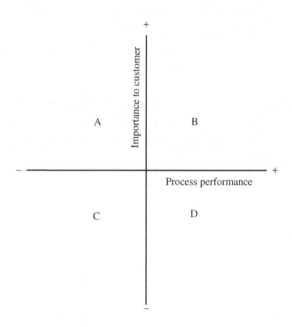

Figure 7.   Matrix of customer importance versus process performance

The use of such a matrix may help to avoid the common problem of continuing to improve in areas that a company is already strong in, or to prevent working on something that is not important to the customer. Improvement should focus on quadrant A where the customer's need is important, but the current process is performing poorly as compared to competitors.

Value-Added Analysis
This technique involves identifying different types of activities within the processes.

Value-added activities: an activity will add value if it satisfies all three of the following requirements:

(a) Customer is willing to pay for the activity
(b) Activity physically changes the product or service
(c) Activity is performed correctly the first time it is undertaken

Control activities: activities required by businesses for risk control but not necessarily value adding to customers. Examples of such control activities include auditing, approving, and reviewing applications.

Non-value added activities: activities that do not add value to the final output. Examples of such activities include moving, filing, and storing documents. Recording the average cost for each activity permits ranking non-value added activities by cost incurred.

In addition, one can easily develop summary statistics showing the percentage devoted to each of the three categories: value added, control, and non-value added activities. It is important to eliminate non-value added activities as well as control activities whenever possible to improve the process performance since these activities do not provide value for the customer and yet add cost to the operations.

Quality Analysis and Benchmarking
This technique involves understanding how the processes are satisfying customers. Some of the questions used in this analysis include:

• Do the processes meet conformance standards?
• How reliable are the processes?

- What is the competence of the staff?
- How do customers respond to the service provided?

Benchmarking is about comparing the firm's or process's activities and performance with what others are doing within the same company, in the same industry, or across industries. Every benchmarking relationship involves two parties:

- The initiator firm which initiates contact and observes
- The target firm (or benchmark) which is being observed

The main purpose of benchmarking is to assess the firm's or process's performance relative to the competition and to identify performance gaps and goals. The underlying idea is to learn and be inspired by the best.

Chapter 6

SUPPLY CHAIN PROCESS REDESIGN FOR DIGITAL TRANSFORMATION

Designing new processes is more of an art than science; it cannot be achieved through a formalized method. Most existing processes were not designed; they just emerged as new parts were iteratively added to satisfy immediate needs. The end result of any such design is very much dependent on the order in which information becomes available. Inefficient processes are thus created when iterative design methods are applied. A new design for the selected supply chain process is derived based on opportunities for improvement identified in process analysis. Major concerns about feasibility and acceptability are also taken into consideration.

One of the most important activities for process redesign with a digital transformation perspective will be to ensure focused workshops with process owners from business are carried out to run through findings, hypotheses, improvement areas, and possible benefits. During these workshops, the program team validates the hypotheses and improvement areas with business process owners and function heads in the steering Committee to gain alignment and agreement. These sessions are very critical and should be detail oriented. Each opportunity must be evaluated against ease of implementation and hard financial benefits in the form of working capital or revenue impact. The program core team has a very

Table 1.   5W2H framework

5W2H	Improvement Dimension	Description
What?	Subject Matter	What is being done in this activity? Can this part of the process be eliminated if it is a waste?
Why?	Purpose	Why is this activity needed? Clarify the purpose of the activity and the overall process.
Who?	People	Who is performing this activity? Are they the best fit for the required role? Could/Should someone else perform the activity?
When?	Sequence	When is the best time to perform this activity? Does it have to be done at a certain specific time of day?
Where?	Location	Where is this activity carried out? Does it have to be done at this location only?
How?	Method	How is the activity carried out? Is this the best way or are there alternatives?
How Much?	Cost	How much does it currently cost? What would be the projected cost after improvement?

important role to play in terms of removing conflicts and ensuring that all stakeholder groups arrive at an agreement on improvement opportunities.

A good starting point for supply chain improvements is the 5W2H framework, as shown in Table 1. 5W2H is a good tool that provides guiding questions when assessing a process. The five Ws — who, what, when, where, and why, and the two Hs — how and how much, force us to consider various facets of the situation being analyzed. It can also be used to understand an existing process before it is redesigned.

Transformation is concerned with changing old ways of doing and thinking, and to achieve this, assumptions will need to be surfaced and challenged. At first sight, it seems easy to say that one will use the customer's needs as a benchmark when deciding what changes to make. But who is the customer (using the 5W2H framework), and are the assumptions made about what the customer wants or needs reasonable? The perceived customer is not necessarily coincident with the real customer. It is likely that there will be many stakeholders involved and the most important stakeholder is not necessarily the ultimate customer. Furthermore, assumptions tend to persist long after they are no longer true and are "invisible" unless a deliberate attempt is made to identify and examine them. Outdated assumptions are a major obstacle to making radical changes in the way we do things.

After identifying potential customers through stakeholder analysis, it is then important to question the assumptions that have been made by supply chain partners. In some cases, it is not necessary to ask the customer what they want. Team members will instead need to make some assumptions about what they think is important to their customers. After surfacing all possible assumptions, the next step is to validate the assumptions in today's context and to generate new ideas through brainstorming to improve the process performance if those assumptions are still valid today.

Brainstorming is one method to keep ideas flowing fast and freely. It is a lateral thinking process and is designed to help individuals break out of their thinking patterns into new ways of looking at things. It works by focusing on the issues faced in the digital supply chain transformation or the outdated assumptions identified, and then coming up with many radical solutions. Ideas should deliberately be as broad and odd as possible.

Group brainstorming can be very effective as it uses the experience and creativity of all members of the group. When individual members reach their limit on an idea, another member's creativity and experience can take the idea to the next stage. Therefore, group brainstorming tends to develop ideas in more depth than individual brainstorming.

During brainstorming sessions, there should be no criticism of ideas. You are trying to open up possibilities and break down wrong assumptions about the limits of the process. Judgments and analysis at this stage will stunt idea generation. Ideas should only be evaluated once the brainstorming session has finished, but do not spend time embellishing ideas or trying to build complete solutions. Valuable but unusual suggestions may appear stupid at first sight. As such, care must be taken to ensure some team members do not crush these new ideas and leave others feeling embarrassed.

Below are 11 redesign principles commonly used for transforming supply chain processes.

Principle 1. Organize Work Around Outcomes not Tasks

We need to focus on horizontal integration of activities. We should eliminate unnecessary handoff and control steps and reduce the need for extensive interfacing with other supply chains. Process transformation teams need to keep in mind that process complexity is reduced while activity complexity grows. An example for such redesign is the integrated import and export process in Singapore with the help of information technology (IT) to interface with all parties in the supply chain, as shown in Figure 8.

Principle 2. Let Those Who Use the Process Perform the Process

The fundamental questions to ask here are, can the company take on more work presently undertaken by customers or suppliers? Would customers or suppliers mind taking up some work presently undertaken by the company? An example of such redesign includes supplier-managed inventory, as shown in Figure 9. In this case, the manufacturer will plan and replenish the stocks on behalf of the retailer to ensure that the goods are always available on the shelf. Sales forecast will improve as the manufacturer will be using the retailer's point of sales data instead of the anticipated sales from the retailer.

Principle 3. Capture Information Once — At the Source

As mentioned earlier, the importance of accuracy in information or data is especially high when we are executing process redesign for the purpose of digital transformation of the supply chain. Identifying the original source of information and capturing it from there reduces costly re-entry and frequent cleansing or processing of erroneous data. Doing it this way will speed up the overall process, increase the quality of information, and reduce costs. An example of such redesign includes the re-export process, as shown in Figure 10. In this case, the information obtained from import

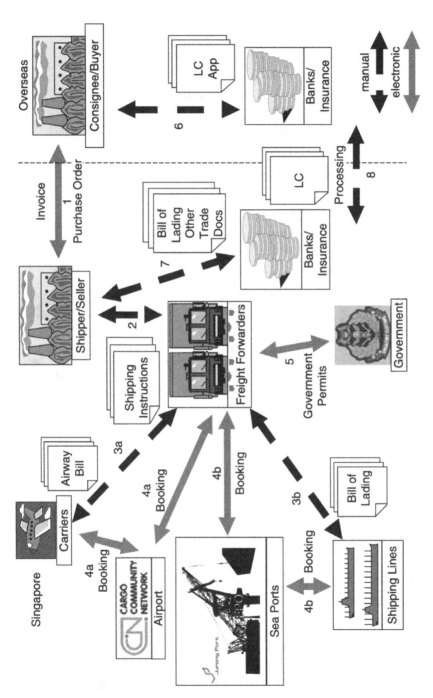

Figure 8. Integrated import and export process in Singapore

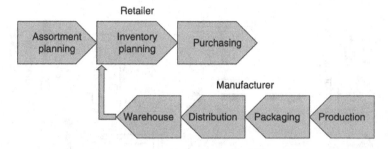

Figure 9.   Vendor managed inventory for retailer

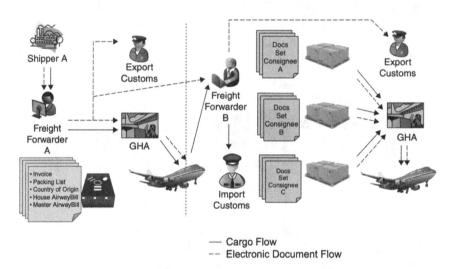

Figure 10.   Re-export process

documentation is reused to prepare export documentation since 70% to 80% of the information is similar.

Principle 4. Put the Decision Point Where the Work is Performed and Build Control in the Process

Essentially, with improved visibility of processes and operations to different levels of process owners and business management, the topic of empowered decision-making has gained significant importance in the last few years. Companies can look at this perspective as an important principle of process transformation by determining the extent to which operational workers take over part of management responsibilities. This helps to answer if and how processes can be integrated horizontally and employee empowerment integrated vertically. From an efficiency or productivity standpoint, we could rationalize whether there is a need for an individual to coordinate the tasks undertaken by several specialists.

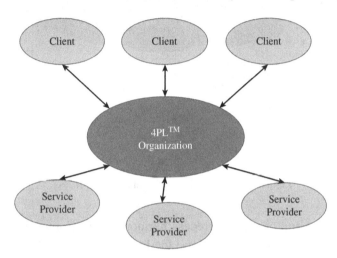

Figure 11. Fourth-party logistics organization

An example of such redesign includes a fourth-party logistics provider (4PL) who manages the performance of third-party service providers to achieve continuous improvement, as shown in Figure 11. In this case, 4PL is the single interface to clients and logistics service providers to ensure that the services offered are matched with clients' expectations. From a process perspective, this is a leading practice that becomes the foundation for digital supply chain collaboration.

Principle 5. Treat Geographically Dispersed Resources as Though They Were Centralized

Technology has been breaking down geographical barriers through virtual co-location with supply chain partners. Geographically distributed resources should not constrain the operational team to only consider

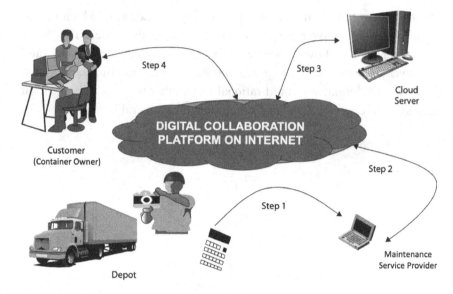

Figure 12.   Container depot global repair process

decentralized approaches to process harmonization. Companies need to leverage digital information and use the Internet as a powerful engine for digital collaboration to break geographical barriers. An example of such redesign includes the depot repair operations for used containers, as shown in Figure 12. In this case, the damages on the container are captured digitally and stored in a cloud server, and the owner of the container can approve or reject the repair immediately. All parties collaborate information in real time to maximize efficiency in the process.

Principle 6. Link or Convert Sequential Activities into Parallel Activities

If sequential activities are operated independently, operational errors may not be detected until the end of the process. Parallel activities reduce delay and overall lead time. The concept of leveraging historical patterns by extensive process data mining has evolved in recent times into a digital value-stream mapping exercise that helps companies eliminate waste in processes and optimize lead times. An example of such redesign includes

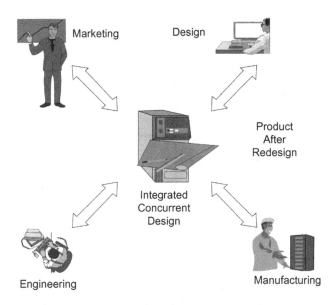

Figure 13. Concurrent product design

concurrent product design, as shown in Figure 13. In this case, new product development can be achieved concurrently by various departments, including the customers and suppliers.

Principle 7. Design Process for the Dominant Flow, not for the Exceptions

The concept of process mining has evolved multiple times with the advent of technology-based enablers. Advanced process mining techniques nowadays capture dominant flows by running through years of historical transaction data from an enterprise resource planning (ERP) system. Once the baseline process flow is established based on the dominant flow, further value addition will include designing separate processing streams for different transaction types (e.g. different needs, complexities, exceptions, etc.). The key benefit of this principle is that it helps to reduce the risk of fragmentation and overly complex processes with inherent coordination problems. An example of such redesign includes designing service

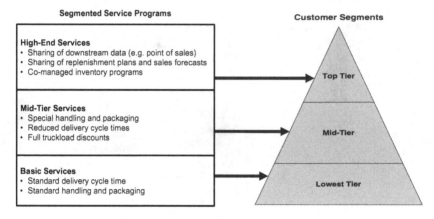

Figure 14.   Differentiated services for each customer segment

programs for different customer segments, as shown in Figure 14. Each customer segment has its own service expectation and needs to be fulfilled by contextualized services.

Principle 8. Look for Ways to Postpone the Final Product

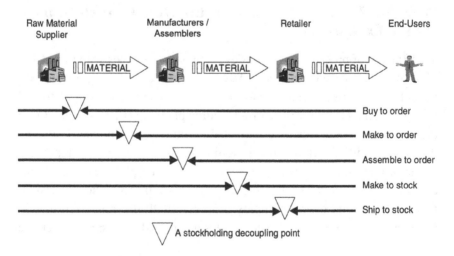

Figure 15.   Postponement strategy for different types of products

In the last few decades, exemplary leading businesses in different industry sectors have successfully practiced "postponement" in manufacturing strategy, also known as "delayed differentiation". Essentially, this strategy involves delaying the final product form as late as possible to reduce inventory and forecast errors. The manufacturing company would keep the product or service in generic form and customize it when the customer confirms the order. An example of such redesign includes paint retailers keeping generic white master batch and blending the chosen color to match each customer requirement on the spot, as shown in Figure 15. In this case, the retailer will not have to keep every product's stock-keeping unit and color listed in the brochure but still be able to blend any color that the customer wants as long as the color pigment is available. Thus, postponement will reduce inventory costs and increase the customer service level at the same time.

Principle 9. Exploit Resource Pooling to Avoid Suboptimization

Companies can consolidate resource requirements to achieve economies of scale. Resource pooling will result in reduced inventory holding costs and improved forecast accuracy. An example of such process redesign includes centralizing the procurement process in hospitals, as shown in

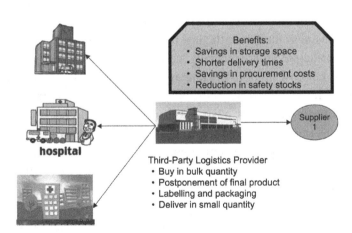

Figure 16. Resource pooling by centralizing procurement process

Figure 16. In this case, the hospitals will outsource the procurement of supplies to a third-party logistics provider, who will procure in bulk quantities and customize the products for these hospitals. Furthermore, hospitals will convert their storerooms into wards, thus generating more revenues.

Principle 10. Avoid Duplicating Tasks with Supply Chain Partners

With the advent of collaborative thinking across supply chain partners in different forms during the last few decades, companies and their supply chain partners should be reviewing how work should be shared across their collaborative functions so that redundancies or duplication are eliminated. The key guiding principle to make this a win-win for both partners is to carry out work where it makes the most sense to do it. An example of such redesign includes the elimination of quality control in a just-in-time production system. In this case, only the supplier will perform the quality check and send the raw material directly to the customer's production floor. The results from the quality check are sent to the manufacturer for process and quality control.

Principle 11. Outsource Non-Core Processes

The outstanding success of business process outsourcing as a concept, and also as a business model, in the last three decades or so definitely underlines this principle. Fundamentally, companies can start with outsourcing processes that cost more to operate as compared to other service providers. More importantly, it helps the company to tap into external expertise that the company does not own. Another criteria could be, if demand for a company's selling products is uncertain or fluctuating while the product has a stable consumption pattern at the market level, outsource the manufacturing process to another supplier who can scale up or down their operations according to the demand pattern or who are also supplying as contract manufacturers to the company's peers.

An example of such redesign includes digital archival of records in medical or law companies, as shown in Figure 17. In this case, the hard

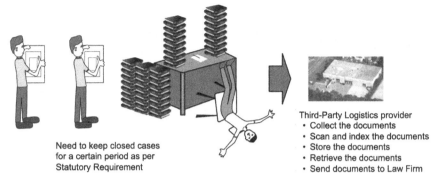

Need to keep closed cases
for a certain period as per
Statutory Requirement

Third-Party Logistics provider
• Collect the documents
• Scan and index the documents
• Store the documents
• Retrieve the documents
• Send documents to Law Firm

Figure 17. Digital archival of records for compliance

copies are scanned and indexed for searching purposes, and these hard copies are then moved to another location with lower storage costs. This process will speed up the document search and reduce the storage costs of documents since most of these companies operate in expensive downtown premises.

Finally, for the implementation of the new process design, a detailed plan should be developed for moving the supply chain process from its present state to that envisioned in the new process design.

This is when the program core team will classify all improvement opportunities and associated process redesign initiatives into quick wins, tactical gains, and strategic success opportunities, as explained in Chapter 3. The next step is prioritization of these initiatives and detailed business case preparation for each business opportunity. The recommended time period is to draw a five-year roadmap and timeline for realizing all the identified business benefits of the digital supply chain transformation program. In a later chapter of this book, readers will find a case study of a specialist patient clinic which successfully applied concepts discussed in this chapter to drive processes transformation and thereby improve efficiency and effectiveness in operations.

Chapter 7

IMPLEMENTING THE DIGITAL SUPPLY CHAIN TRANSFORMATION

Having successfully redesigned supply chain processes with an alignment to a digital future, the actual implementation of process changes and technology solutions begins. It is imperative to consider four different dimensions coming together for the successful implementation of the digital strategy. The first dimension is related to business processes and the second is concerned with structures of jobs and the people needed to fill them. The third area of interaction refers to the role of managers, the working relationships, and the measurement systems, and, finally, the fourth dimension is related to employees' values and beliefs. Consequently, transforming a company's processes affects all aspects of that company, as shown in Figure 18.

The implementation of digital supply chain transformation is then carried out by the following activities.

Defining New Organizational Structure

The new process design for the organization should include necessary job positions, required skills and knowledge, number of people required to fill these positions, workgroups and teams, and the most effective supporting management structure. In principle, if these steps are followed, then an ideal (e.g. properly fitting) organization can be designed for transformed

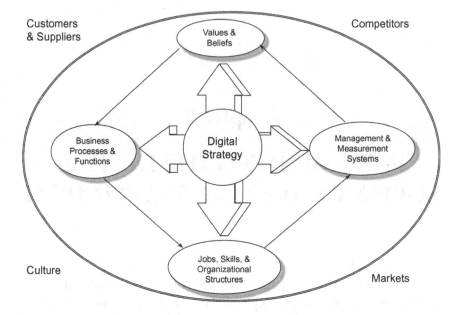

Figure 18. Alignment for successful digital strategy

supply chain processes. The organization structure should have the following characteristics:

- Minimal number of interfaces to suppliers and customers
- Optimal span of control for the number of direct reports per manager, given the type of work
- Minimal number of layers
- Clear roles and responsibilities
- The avoidance of overlapping or fuzzy responsibilities

According to the advocates of digital supply chain transformation, modern organizations must abandon the old control mechanisms that characterize the hierarchical and bureaucratic organization as these control mechanisms are obsolete. There are three reasons to support this claim. First, digitally-enabled information systems, expert systems, and decision-support systems can provide workers with information that enables them to make better decisions themselves. It is no longer necessary to separate thought and action. Decisions should be made where the work is performed.

Second, the modern workforce is well-educated and capable of assuming responsibility. Modern workers expect more autonomy and self-control and, moreover, expect to have a say in how a supply chain is run. People do not want to simply follow rules; they want to make their own rules and decisions. Third, the supply chain environment has changed. It is much more dynamic and competitive than before. The old bureaucratic system, which was geared towards efficiency and control, is out of place in an age where flexibility, variety, and customer satisfaction are the keys to success. It is necessary to design organizations that mirror the increased differentiation of consumer demand, and the flexibility and power of the technology.

One important element for any transformative thinking is the role of management. Digital supply chain transformation emphasizes the value of reducing management levels and the number of managers within organizations. Hierarchical structures should be flattened, and a manager should have a greater span of control. In addition, the role of managers should be changed. A manager should become a consultant, advisor, and coach, and not necessarily a supervisor and controller. Workers should manage and control themselves. The job of a manager is to help their employees to do richer and more demanding work.

Since processes cross-functional borders, the traditional department structure is becoming obsolete for a transformed organization. Instead, people will be organized in multidisciplinary teams. These teams could replace the functional department structure, and each member in the process team is "collectively responsible for process results".

Redefining Performance Measurement

Performance measurements will have to align to the new process in order for workers to change to the new process. Otherwise, they will soon revert to their old process. Tables 2, 3, and 4 show role-wise process flow for the application of a business license in Singapore, followed by the performance measurement for each department, and finally the measurement for each job and its target setting.

Table 2.   Process representation by roles

Process Name: Business License Application				
Customer	**Processing Officer**	**Approving Officer**	**Clerk**	**IT System**
1. Submit application				
	2a. Review application			2b. Check rules for compliance
		3a. Approve application		3b. Check rules for approval
			4. Print license and bill customer	
	5. Inform customer			
6. Customer receives license				

Table 3.   Performance targets for functions across processes

Targets for Activity Within Each Department or Function						
Major Processes	**Processing Department**		**Audit Department**		**Finance Department**	
Step	Output	Target	Output	Target	Output	Target
License application	Application reviewed	1 day	Application audited	2 days	Customer billed	10 days

Table 4.   Performance measurement criterion/targets for processes

Job Targets for Activity			
Output	**Critical Dimension**	**Measurement**	**Target**
License application for review	Accuracy	% of errors	1%
	Timeliness	% within 1 day	95%

Evaluating and Defining Implementation Options

Having designed and tested the new process, an organization will be faced with considerable challenge of migrating from the current process environment to the radically new design. A full "cutover" may be difficult or impossible. If the new process involves customers, revenue, or valued employees, or if the process change will be highly visible internally or externally, the firm may not want to risk a full, abrupt transition. Alternatives to full cutover include a phased introduction, creating a pilot, or creating an entirely new business unit.

A pilot is a smaller scale, but fully operational, implementation of a new process in a relatively small unit of the organization based on a particular geography, product, or set of customers. Although pilots are often viewed as a means of testing a new process (or other type of intervention), the goal should be to achieve success rather than a merely objective test. Thus, the unit selected should be the one most capable of achieving successful change.

Another approach is to begin with a pilot and follow with a phase by phase implementation. A company might, for example, implement new system capabilities and skills as they become available. A phased approach may be the most economically feasible, in that companies can derive some financial benefit from the process change earlier than might otherwise be possible, but it is not necessarily less disruptive than a full cutover. In fact, the sense of constant change and instability may be difficult for some employees to handle. At this stage it is prudent to also evaluate all potential initiatives or projects identified for setting up the digital supply chain transformation, in a scientific way, considering each initiative's impact.

This step involves selecting one or more identified initiatives/projects based on their impact on customers and the organization. The decision is not to reject or eliminate alternatives, but to establish priorities instead. All identified initiatives/projects could be impactful, but they must prioritized because of the limited amount of resources available. The objective of this step is thus to allow the team involved to obtain a consensus on which proposed initiatives/projects (or ideas) must be given what priority.

Before the evaluation can start, staff participating in the evaluation and selection process must share a clear vision of the ideas to be evaluated:

objectives, implications, feasibilities, etc. The selection criteria must be established for evaluation and are built on three dimensions: customer benefits, organization benefits, and aversion factor. Criteria for customer benefits include improving quality and effectiveness; increased speed, responsiveness, and reduced wait; and enhancing convenience, accessibility, and comfort. Criteria for organization benefits include operational savings, increased productivity and efficiency, increased capacity, strategic advantage, and enhanced image and reputation.

Aversion factor relates to the negative impact of an initiative or project that reduces its attractiveness. Criteria for aversion factors include cost of implementing the project, difficulty of implementing the project, and risk of implementing the project.

Once the staff have set the criteria to evaluate each project, they add weightage to each criterion from 0 to 1 based on importance. The coordinator (person leading the evaluation process) will then ask the team members to score each project against each attribute for customer and organization benefits based on a score of -3 to 3 (-3 denotes erosion of contribution, 0 denotes no effect, and 3 denotes significant contribution). In the case of the aversion factor, the scoring is based on a score of -3 to 0 since all the

	Customer Benefits				Organizational Benefits						Aversion Factors			
Options	Quality/ Effectiveness	Speed/ Responsiveness	Convenience/ Accessibility	Others	Operational Savings	Productivity /Efficiency	Capacity	Strategic Advantage	Image	Others	Implementation Costs	Difficulty	Risk	Others

Figure 19.   Template to evaluate initiatives/projects for digital supply chain transformation

criteria refer to the negative impact of performance. Figure 19 shows a template that can be used by staff to conduct the evaluation. The team members understand that this is not a scientific tool. Rather, it is based on individual opinion and its strength lies in its simplicity. Even though the criteria are clear, the projects defined are not easy for comparison and, in this case, more deliberation about each project does not necessarily produce better results. For the rating of each attribute, every participant must question the impact each project has against the rest.

Once the staff have classified all the ideas against every criterion, the coordinator will then create a final table recording the total score of each project. Using the final score, average the score and multiple by each criterion's weight (if any), and add the result for each column to compute the weighted score or each project.

After these steps are taken, they now have some quantitative evaluation of the projects against each criterion that are deemed important. Therefore, they have passed from individual and subjective perceptions to common numeric conclusions. Now it is time to study the values obtained in the tables.

Finalizing Enabling Digital Technologies

Technology is essential for the new process so that it can meet the digital transformation objectives and goals. Examples of how technologies can help in transforming processes are shown in Table 5.

Identification, evaluation, and adoption of digital enablers further helps in achieving the supply chain transformation vision. The ability of the new supply chain process design to meet its performance targets and yield its expected business benefits is possible by applying the latest digital technology to the new process. During detailed process design, determining the types of technologies that are required to support the new business processes is needed. The following example will illustrate how to exploit potential digital levers to support each activity in the new process. This illustration involves importers who are importing poultry into a country from overseas. Importers can obtain the import permit from a government agency once their poultry pass the inspection test. The key activities involved in the application for the poultry import permit, in this case, are shown in Figure 20.

Table 5.   Digital technologies for enabling supply chain processes (McKinsey, 2016)

Old Rule	Digital Enabler	New Perspective
Information can appear in only one place at a time	Cloud Application	Information can appear simultaneously in as many places as needed
Only experts can perform complex work	Artificial Intelligence	A generalist may be able to do the work of an expert system
Businesses must choose between centralization and decentralization	5G Telecommunication networks	Businesses can simultaneously reap the benefits of centralization and decentralization
Managers make all decisions	Big Data	Decision making is part of data analytics
Field personnel need offices — where to receive, store, retrieve and transmit information	Wireless communication and Mobile applications	Field personnel can send and receive information on the go, anytime, anywhere
The last contact with a potential buyer is personal contact	Interactive chatbot	The best contact with a potential buyer is effective dialogue
People must find where things are	Internet of things	IoT tell you where they are
Plans get revised periodically	High performance computing	Plans can get revised instantaneously

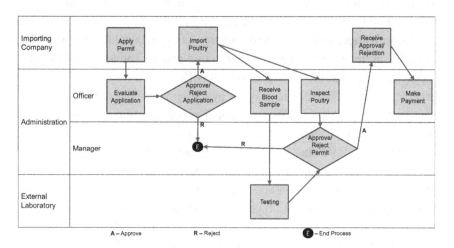

Figure 20.   Import process for poultry

Table 6. Identifying Digital enablers for value-add activities

Key Activities	Value-add Activity?	Potential Digital/Technology Application (If Any)
Apply for poultry permit	Value add	Online or mobile channels
Evaluate application	Value add	Verify with database of countries banned from import of poultry using blockchan
Approve or reject application.	Value add	Online or mobile channels
Import poultry	Not applicable	Not applicable
Inspect poultry for disease and other potential infection	Non-value add	Internet of Things (IoT)
Draw blood sample for the lab	Non-value add	Not applicable
Test blood sample for infection	Value add	Extract test procedures from laboratory information management system using TOT Link testing equipment with laboratory information management system to update test results
Make decision (approve or reject permit)	Value add	Decision support tool to assist manager to approve permit based on blood sample result and inspection result
Inform applicant of the outcome	Value add	Online or mobile channels
Collect payment	Non-value add	Using e-banking or VISA

These activities can be classified as value adding or non-value adding, and potential digitalization can be identified for each activity, as shown in Table 6.

As a result of this exercise, four potential levels of technology and digital enablement are identified for this process. They are as follows:

- An enterprise system on the cloud to store and retrieve information regarding the test procedures and test results
- An advanced predictive analytics-based decision support tool to assist the manager in approving permits

- An online or mobile connection to the enterprise system to request for testing
- An online payment system linking to the enterprise system

While the identification of digital technology enablers for the new process is critical, one needs to be mindful in terms of the benefits or value in implementing such technology to support the new process. Keeping in mind how expensive the cost of digitalization can be, it is imperative to look upon technology not only for the benefits provided to the customer, but also how large its contribution will be on process performance. Through the application of a simple assessment test, one would be prevented from the fallacy of rushing into a passion for an information technology application that might be futile for the organization.

A simple assessment test for illustration is the example of an automatic teller machine (ATM) technology in serving its customers. An initial problem faced is how to be able to serve customers at any time, and ATMs make it possible to serve customers outside office hours. Some of the questions that need to be addressed to justify this technology include: how much manpower is needed for processing cash replenishment? How much is the financial profit derived from utilizing ATMs? What are the targets, set in numerical terms, for the growth of funds and the increase of the customer base that are expected to be derived from employing ATM services? How large is the actual number of potential customers wishing to conduct transactions outside office hours? How about the stock management of customer ATM cards?

By raising these critical questions, the impact of applying ATM technology becomes clearer, e.g. whether the ease provided to customers for fund withdrawal conflicts with any potential problems concerning bank liquidity and third-party funds. When all these questions have been answered, the results will make clear whether there is a real need for the application of ATMs at the present moment to support the new process, or other alternatives should be considered.

Chapter 8

SUPPLY CHAIN TRANSFORMATIONS IN THE HEALTHCARE INDUSTRY

In this chapter, we will discuss two unique case studies, both pertaining to the healthcare industry. The first case study that follows focuses on the highly strategic importance of business process analysis and redesign as precursors to any digital initiative towards a larger supply chain transformation.

Case Study 1: Transforming the Reverse Logistics Operations for a Medical Equipment Company

This project involves a factory based in Bangkok with products distributed through their central distribution center located in Bangkok. Customer orders are fulfilled based on the geographical location of customers. For customers in Bangkok, the company will use its own truck to deliver the order to the retailer. For customers in other provinces, the selected means of transportation will depend on the volume of the order. If the volume is large enough for a full truckload (FTL), the company will use its own truck to deliver the order. However, if the order is less than truckload (LTL), a third-party transportation service provider will be used to deliver the order. The lead time for delivery is dependent upon truck routing, scheduling, availability, as well as final destinations.

Customers can use the company's reverse logistics channel to repair their products. However, customers will be required to send the products to the main service center based in Bangkok for repair. The regional service center and retailer are only capable of being used as a consolidation point to send the products back to the Bangkok center. Another difficulty is the low frequency and lack of trucks that are returning to the Bangkok service center. These issues result in a long lead time before any repairs can be done to the faulty products. The process map (see Figure 21) depicts the swim-lane diagram for original reverse logistics process.

Under the original reverse logistics channel structure, the company had received many complaints on repair service lead time caused by long periods of waiting time. Another problem was the costs of transport (to and from the manufacturer), which are considered a burden for both the company and its customers. It is normal practice for the company to pay a third-party transportation service provider for returning a product from its retailer to its service center. Customers also had to bear freight charges from the Bangkok service center to their home as the manufacturer does not pay for these charges. The only solution for the customer was to collect the goods himself at the Bangkok service center. The lead time comparison for returns in Bangkok, other provinces with full load, and less than full load trucking can be seen in Table 7.

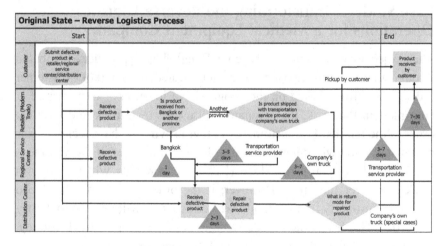

Figure 21.   Original process flow

Table 7. Lead time comparison for returns in Bangkok and outside Bangkok

	From Bangkok	From Other Provinces	From Other Provinces
Retailer to Service Center	1 day	3 to 7 days (company's truck)	3 to 5 days (third-party transport)
Time Spent at Service Center	2 to 3 days	2 to 3 days	2 to 3 days
Time Spent at Service Shop	N/A	N/A	N/A
Service Center to Customer	3 to 7 days	7 to 30 days (company's truck)	3 to 7 days (National Postal Service)
Total Lead Time	6 to 11 days	12 to 40 days	8 to 15 days

In this company, the only difference in cost that can be quantified is the transportation costs for the company's major products: laboratory equipment and electrocardiogram (ECG) equipment. The transportation costs for these two products back to the central service center in Bangkok, by the company's own truck, are US$0.20 and US$0.79 per box, respectively, and US$0.75 and US$1.75 per box, respectively, if a third-party service provider is involved. In addition, the costs of freight to return the repaired products to customers are US$2.50 and US$3.75 per box, respectively. Returns are usually sent through the National Postal Service. Table 8 provides a comparison in terms of annual cost involved with regards to the transportation of returned items.

The company has set up a centralized service center to support returned products in order to keep their costs down. However, the most frequently cited problem with a centralized service center is the relatively poor level of customer service. In order to cope with return uncertainty and provide good customer service, some companies have tried to increase their ability, flexibility, and agility to respond to customer needs against a backdrop of increasing customer service cost. One way is to set up service centers near customers, in contrast to near the main factory or main distribution center, that could be able to help minimize customers inconvenience in terms of time and cost involved with regards to access to after-sales or repair services. However, this will increase their reverse logistics

Table 8.   Annual transportation cost based on existing reverse logistics process

Item	Laboratory Equipment	ECG Equipment
Number of products sold annually	300,000	10,000
Average number of products returned and repaired at service shop	N/A	N/A
Average number of products returned to service center	10,000	300
— via customer	1,000	30
— via company's own truck	7,000	210
— via transportation service provider	2,000	60
Costs of using company's own truck	US$0.20 per box	US$0.79 per box
Costs charged by transportation service provider	US$0.75 per box	US$1.75 per box
Total costs for product returned to service center	US$2,900	US$271
Subtotal	**US$3,171**	
Average number of repaired products returned to customers	10,000	300
— via customer pick-up at service shop	N/A	N/A
— via customer pick-up at service center	1,000	30
— via shipment by National Postal Service	9,000	270
Costs charged by National Postal Service (freight collected)	US$2.50 per box	US$3.75 per box
Number of repaired products shipped from service center to service shop	N/A	N/A
Costs of using company's own truck	US$0.20 per box	US$0.79 per box
Total costs for product returned to customers	US$22,500	US$1,013
Subtotal	**US$23,513**	
Total annual cost of transportation in the reverse logistics process	**US$26,684**	

costs. A three–phase methodology was followed to define the supply chain process transformation needed.

Phase 1: Project Initiation

Vision	A highly responsive reverse logistics center for after-sales
Goal	Short response time without increasing reverse logistics costs
Target	• Reduce respond time by 70% • Reduce operations costs by 50%
Team members	Staff from operations, customers, transportation, third-party logistics, etc.

Time analysis for original process

Time taken to collect, repair, and return to customers was too long. Customers expect shorter duration regardless of location.

- Time taken to collect, repair, and return the defective equipment to customers in Bangkok was taking about 6 to 11 days
- Time taken to collect, repair, and return the defective equipment to customers in other provinces would take about 12 to 40 days

Cost analysis for original process

Customers are not willing to pay for the transport cost from the service center back to their home. Neither are they willing to pay to collect it from the service center themselves.

- Cost to collect the defective equipment from the customer and deliver it to the service center is US$0.20 to US$0.79 using the company's own truck and US$0.75 to US$1.75 using a third-party truck
- Cost to deliver the repaired equipment back to the customer is US$0.20 to US$0.79 using the company's own truck and US$2.50 to US$3.75 using the National Postal Service

Quality analysis for current process

Customers complained about the poor level of service using the centralized service center. Sometimes the repair quality gets affected during transportation from centralized service center. The turnaround time is long and customers are not willing to collect the equipment after it has been repaired.

Phase 2: Challenge Assumptions to Generate Ideas

Organization		
Assumptions	**Challenges**	**Ideas**
Defective equipment are cheaper to repair than replace	Some of the equipment are cheaper to be replaced	Replace obsolete equipment with new models
Centralized service center will save repair costs	Transportation cost can increase the overall repair cost	Explore decentralized service center
Centralized service center will have all the necessary equipment	Some tests can be performed with commonly available equipment	Explore decentralized service center for those tests
It is cheaper to outsource transportation to third party	Transportation providers charge much more than the cost to use in-house trucking	Consider buying a fleet of trucks for better control

Customer		
Assumptions	**Challenges**	**Ideas**
Customers are willing to pay for transporting their equipment back to their home	Customers expect the company to send the equipment back to them for free	Customers can pick up the equipment from a nearby store
Customers are willing to collect the equipment from the service center	Customers expect the company to deliver the equipment back to them	Customers can pick up the equipment from a nearby store or 7-Eleven convenience store

(Continued)

	Customer	
Assumptions	**Challenges**	**Ideas**
Customers are willing to wait two to three weeks for the equipment to be repaired	Customers expect faster turnaround time to repair their equipment	Improve the repair process
Equipment belonging to customers outside Bangkok take a longer time to be repaired	All customers expect their equipment to be repaired as soon as possible regardless of location	Treat all customers the same regardless of location

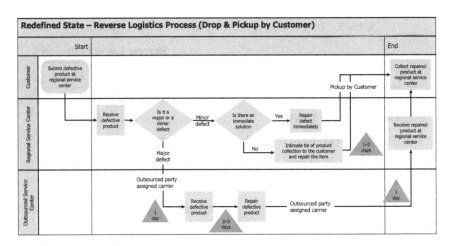

Figure 22. Redefined process with self-drop and pickup by customer

Phase 3: Process Selection and Transformation

In order to improve efficiency of the manufacturer's reverse logistics channel, the redefined processes, as shown in Figures 22 and 23, are proposed. Under the future reverse logistics process, the manufacturer establishes service shops in all the retailers' outlets. These service shops serve as decoupling points for customers' demand fluctuation. In conjunction with the establishment of service shops, a blockchain system is also proposed to keep track of all information updates such as the demand and

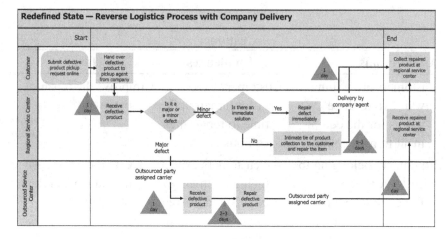

Figure 23.   Redefined process with company delivery

Table 9.   Impact of re-engineering on reverse logistic process

Item	Reverse Logistics Process	
	Current	Future
Annual Transportation Cost of Returned Product	US$26,684	US$224
Customer Satisfaction Level	Low	High
Responsiveness to Customer Demand	Low	High
Lead Time for Product Repair (for 95% of cases)	6 to 40 days	1 day

inventory level for each spare part in total and at each service shop, order quantity and lead time to arrive, etc.

In the redefined reverse logistics process, 95%of the returned products are being repaired at the service shop, which eliminates most of the transportation. The rest of the returned items are being sent to the central service center in Bangkok if they are considered difficult cases and lead time is less critical. Table 9 illustrates the impact of applying re-engineering to the reverse logistics process.

The future state reverse logistics process will help to alleviate existing problems such as long lead time for repairs. In most cases, returned products can be repaired at service shops. This will lead to the reduction of lead time and waiting time as shown in Table 10.

Table 10. Lead time comparison before and after re-engineering

| | Current Process | | New Process | | | |
| | | | Customer Self Drop and Pickup | | Company Pickup and Delivery | |
	Bangkok	Other Provinces	Repair at Regional Service Center/Shop	Repair at Outsourced Partner	Repair at Regional Service center/Shop	Repair at Outsourced Partner
Transport time from customer to service center	1 day	3–7 days	N/A	N/A	1 day	1 day
Time spent at service center	2–3 days	2–3 days	N/A	N/A	N/A	N/A
Time spent at service shop	N/A	N/A	1–2 days	N/A	1–2 days	N/A
Transport time from service shop to outsourced partner	N/A	N/A	N/A	1 day	N/A	1 day
Time spent at outsourced partner	N/A	N/A	N/A	2–3 days	N/A	2–3 days
Transport time from outsourced partner to service shop/customer	N/A	N/A	N/A	1 day	N/A	1 day
Transport time from service center to customer	3–7 days	7–30 days	N/A	N/A	1 day	N/A
Total lead time	6–11 days	12–40 days	1–2 days	4–5 days	3–4 days	5–6 days
Average lead time	8.5 days	26 days	1.5 days	4.5 days	3.5 days	5.5 days
Time saving in new process (Bangkok)			6 days	4 days	4 days	3 days
Time saving in new process (other province)			24 days	21 days	22 days	20 days

The new process is able to save more than 65% of costs and reduce the lead time to 1 to 3 days as compared to 6 to 40 days with the current process.

In summary, supply chain process assessment for digital transformation should ensure that the program core team has collated structured information and findings from document reviews, detailed process analysis, and stakeholder discussions. We have been able to identify process improvement opportunity areas by benchmarking against industry leading practices. Through a series of brainstorming sessions, we have formulated and created hypotheses for process improvements by digital levers enablement. These hypotheses have been ranked and prioritized based on quantified potential business benefits.

Now we look at another case study wherein more aspects of the digital supply chain transformation (DSCT) have been incorporated. Digital supply chain transformation teams in different companies are encouraged to carry out a comparative exercise of the previous case study and the following one. The previous case study was detailed more in terms of concepts of supply chain process analysis, benchmarking, and redesign. Some of the principles discussed in earlier chapters could well be seen in action. When DSCT teams in organizations read the next case study, they can try and apply principles applied in the previous one to this one, and vice versa.

Case Study 2: Transforming the Outpatient Operations for a Specialist Clinic

A specialist private clinic (SPC) in Singapore was involved in transforming their outpatient process to minimize the waiting time for their patients. Previously, a patient from SPC had to go to different counters for registration of different services within the same hospital. Even if the patient had a prior appointment with the specialist, she/he may need to get an X-ray first. So, she/he has to proceed to the X-ray room, register, and wait for turn. This would have taken at least 30 minutes. After taking the X-ray film, she/he will need to carry the result and wait for her/his turn to see the doctor. This will take another 30 minutes. Upon seeing the doctor, she/he will pay for the consultation and make a new appointment if necessary.

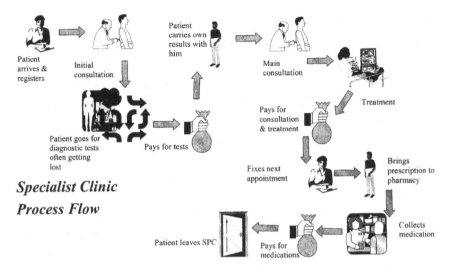

Specialist Clinic
Process Flow

Figure 24. Original process flow for a specialist private clinic

She/he will then carry the doctor's prescription and pass it to the pharmacy for a prescription. She/he ends up spending half a day in the hospital, as illustrated in Figure 24.

Goal Setting and Objectives

The CEO of the SPC initiated this transformation project with the following goals and objectives to enhance its services.

The goal was to design an outpatient process that identifies new outcomes for quality care, patient services, and patient satisfaction. To meet the goal, the following objectives were suggested:

- Radically simplify and streamline functions and processes
- Eliminate routine patient queuing
- Improve overall experience when visiting the SPC

A project team was handpicked by the CEO for this project, consisting of doctors, nurses, and information technology (IT) and related support staff.

Assumption Surfacing

At first sight, it seems easy to say that one will use the customer's needs as a benchmark when deciding what changes to make. But, who is the customer; and are the assumptions made about what the customer wants or needs reasonable? The perceived customer is not necessarily coincident with the real customer. It is likely that there will be many stakeholders involved and the most important stakeholder is not necessarily the ultimate customer.

The staff started identification of stakeholders and the surfacing of assumptions. Assumptions tend to persist long after they are no longer true and are "invisible" unless a deliberate attempt is made to identify and examine them. Outdated assumptions are a major obstacle to making radical changes to the old process. The SPC staff made use of simple templates in surfacing assumptions as shown in the following tables.

WHAT Template
Getting cured is important to our patients
Collecting payment is important to us
Specialized equipment is required for lab tests

WHO Template
A doctor is required to perform diagnosis/prescribe treatment
A patient must be ill before visiting the SPC
A patient must move from one test station to another

WHERE Template
A patient can only be diagnosed at the SPC
A patient must collect medication in person
A doctor must be at the SPC to perform diagnosis/treatment

WHEN Template
A patient must be diagnosed before he can be treated
A patient must undergo initial consultation before taking tests
A patient must pay for consultation/treatment before leaving the SPC

WHY Template
A patient must undergo tests in order to determine his condition
A patient's condition must be known in order to give him treatment
Initial consultation is required to determine what tests are appropriate

HOW Template
A patient can only be diagnosed by going through tests
A patient can only be tested by taking a sample or doing a scan, etc.

These templates are meant as a guide in surfacing assumptions for the staff and need not be used in the strictest manner. It is useful at this stage to include team members who were not involved in this process for assumption surfacing. These members will be able to question very fundamental assumptions that could have been taken for granted by others. These fundamental assumptions can make a quantum improvement to performance if they can be challenged successfully.

Some of the templates were overlapping with perspectives and this is fine as long as they get listed in any of the templates. The decision to include an assumption is to assess if this assumption can be perceived as an obstacle and, if challenged successfully, can achieve the transformation objectives.

After identifying potential customers through stakeholder analysis, it is then important to question the assumptions that have been made about the stakeholder group. In some cases, it is not necessary to ask the customer what they want, and the staff instead are making some assumptions about what they think is important to their customers. Assumption surfacing will bring a further degree of rigor to transformation in the key area of surfacing and challenging assumptions. After surfacing all the assumptions, the next step is to challenge assumptions by staff either in questioning the relevance of these assumptions in today's context or in contradicting them to achieve radical improvement in performance. This is illustrated in the following table.

Table 11. Assumptions and challenges for a private clinic

Assumptions	Challenges
WHAT Template	
Getting cured is important to our patients	• Staying well is important to our patients • Getting cured quickly and with the least cost, risk, and hassle is important to our patients
Collecting payment is important to us	• Being remunerated is important to us — In money? In other terms? From elsewhere? • Continuing to operate and be of service is important to us
Specialized equipment is required for lab tests	• Some tests can be performed with commonly available equipment
WHO Template	
A doctor is required to perform diagnosis/prescribe treatment	• Some diagnoses and treatment prescriptions can be done by other staff/doctors not within the SPC
A specialist technician is required to perform certain tests/scans (e.g., X-rays)	• Certain tests/scans can be performed by ordinary nursing staff or staff not within the SPC
A patient must be ill before visiting the SPC	• A patient can visit the SPC on occasions other than when she/he is ill
A patient must move from one test station to another	• A patient can perform all his tests in one location • A patient's movement through all stations should be minimized • Tests can be brought to the patient • A patient can be moved from one test station to another without effort
WHERE Template	
A patient can only be diagnosed at the SPC	• A patient can be diagnosed at home/a location close to home or conveniently accessible to her/him
A patient can only be treated at the SPC	• A patient can be treated at home/a location close to home or conveniently accessible to him
A patient must collect medication in person	• Medication can be delivered to the patient/collected from a convenient location

Table 11. (*Continued*)

Assumptions	Challenges
A doctor must be at the SPC to perform diagnosis/treatment	• A doctor can diagnose as well as treat patient from another location within or outside the SPC • A doctor can diagnose or treat patient at a time outside of the patient's visit to the SPC
WHEN Template	
A patient must be diagnosed before she/he can be treated	• A patient can be diagnosed and treated at the same time • A patient can be treated without diagnosis
A patient must undergo initial consultation before taking tests	• A patient can take tests without initial consultation
A patient must pay for consultation/treatment before leaving the SPC	• A patient can make payment after leaving the SPC • A patient can make payments in instalments
A patient can only fix the next appointment after paying for treatment and consultation	• A patient can fix the next appointment while paying for treatment/consultation • A patient can fix the next appointment from home (after leaving the SPC)
WHY Template	
Patient records must be retrieved the day before to ensure availability at the SPC on appointment day	• Patient records should be available anytime/all the time
A patient must wait at the clinic so that she/he is available when her/his name is called (for consulting/treatment) so that the SPC's resources are efficiently utilized	• A patient can wait in more pleasant surroundings or do other things while waiting to be called without adversely affecting efficiency
A patient must collect and carry her/his test results with her/him to ensure availability at main consultation	• Test results should be available at main consultation without patient having to carry them along
HOW Template	
A patient can only be diagnosed by going through tests	• A patient can be diagnosed without going through tests/scans
A patient can only be tested by taking a sample or doing a scan etc.	• A patient can be tested remotely • A patient can conduct the test himself

Idea Generation

For each challenge posed, the staff generate as many ideas as possible to satisfy it. Challenges specify what is to be achieved while ideas specify how they are to be achieved. Brainstorming is one method to keep ideas flowing fast and freely. It is a lateral thinking process and is designed to help staff break out of their thinking patterns into new ways of looking at things. It works by focusing on a challenge and then coming up with many radical solutions to it.

During brainstorming sessions, the staff try to open up possibilities and break down assumptions about the limits of the process. Judgments and analysis at this stage will stunt idea generation. Ideas should only be evaluated once the brainstorming session has finished, and they should ensure that they do not spend too much time embellishing ideas or trying to build complete solutions. Valuable but unusual suggestions may appear stupid at first sight. As such, care must be taken to ensure the staff do not crush these new ideas and leave group members feeling embarrassed. Some of the suggestions during the brainstorming session include:

- Relocate work to/from customers/suppliers
  Can the organization do more work on behalf of customers?
  Can the organization get the customers to do some of their work?
  Can the organization do more work on behalf of suppliers?
  Can the organization get the suppliers to do some of their work?
- Minimize interface
  Can interfaces with customers be reduced by automating some of the standard enquiries and simple transactions using automated voice response systems and information kiosks?
- Task compression and integration
  Can hand-offs be reduced so that there will be fewer delays and errors?
- Natural parallelism
  Can activities be done concurrently instead of sequentially?
- Standardization versus diversity
  Can components of products or services be standardized so that they are capable of being combined together to provide products or services with a customer focus?

- Case manager
  Can a disaggregated collection of diverse experts be coordinated together?
- Increased/decreased alternatives
  Can the process be made less complex by varying the number of alternative inputs?
- Early/deferred decision-making
  Can process costs be reduced by changing the sequence of decision-making?

The generated ideas are listed in Table 12.

Table 12. Ideas generated for a private clinic

Assumptions	Challenges	Ideas
WHAT Template		
Getting cured is important to our patients	• Staying well is important to our patients • Getting cured quickly and with the least cost, risk, and hassle is important to our patients	• Establish preventive care program — new line of business • Better patient education and counselling regarding treatment projects
Collecting payment is important to us	• Being remunerated is important to us — in money? In other terms? • Continuing to exist and be of service is important to us	• What are alternative sources of funding to supplement health insurance and patient's own funds? • Continued provision of high standard of affordable health care • Better categorization of patients; ensure each category's needs are adequately met
Specialized equipment is required for lab tests	• Some tests can be performed with commonly available equipment	• Diagnostic test-kits (to allow self-administered tests) — some conditions only; specially created test-kits for the SPC's needs
WHO Template		
A doctor is required to perform diagnosis/prescribe treatment	• Some diagnoses and treatment prescriptions can be done by other staff/doctors not within the SPC	• Phone/electronic (preliminary) consultation with patient's general practitioner (GP) — may eliminate unnecessary referrals, reduce load on the SPC of patients who do not require specialist care. This will also ensure that appropriate specialization is approached for the patient's specific need.

(Continued)

Table 12.   (*Continued*)

Assumptions	Challenges	Ideas
A specialist technician is required to perform certain tests/scans (e.g., X-rays)	• Certain tests/scans can be performed by ordinary nursing staff/ staff not within the SPC	• Allow the patient's GP to collect samples/ perform simple tests on behalf of SPC staff
A patient must be ill before visiting the SPC	• A patient can visit the SPC on occasions other than when he is ill	• Preventive care education — tailored to specific high-risk groups
WHERE Template		
A patient can only be diagnosed at the SPC	• A patient can be diagnosed at home/a location close to home or conveniently accessible to him	• Outsource basic testing to other polyclinics • Establish a "Service Centre" to conduct tests in a more conveniently located place — perhaps a major train station?
A patient can only be treated at the SPC	• A patient can be treated at home/a location close to home or conveniently accessible to him	• The Service Centre can also perform certain types of treatments — for some conditions only • Allow the patient's GP to treat her/him in consultation with the SPC specialist (for follow-up treatment only)
A patient must collect medication in person	• Medication can be delivered to patient/ collected from a convenient location	• "Test lab on wheels" to dispense medication at patient's home • Establish electronic prescription arrangements with major pharmacies — patient only has to go to a pharmacy branch • The Service Centre can also dispense medication
WHEN Template		
A patient must be diagnosed before she/he can be treated	• A patient can be diagnosed and treated at the same time	• Allow the patient's GP to perform "presumptive treatment" under the guidance of the SPC specialist
A patient must undergo initial consultation before taking tests	• A patient can take tests without initial consultation	• Allow the patient's GP to prescribe tests in consultation with the SPC specialist — patient will go for tests on their first SPC visit (without need for initial consultation) • Advisory expert system available on the Internet to replace initial consultation (some conditions only) — to recommend what tests to perform or whether to see specialist first; allow for booking of tests online

Table 12. *(Continued)*

Assumptions	Challenges	Ideas
A patient must pay for consultation/ treatment before leaving the SPC	• A patient can make payment after leaving the SPC • A patient can make payments in instalments	• Patient will be billed later — project for direct charges to credit cards • Establish electronic fund transfer
WHY Template		
Patient records must be retrieved the day before to ensure availability at the SPC on appointment day	• Patient records should be available anytime/all the time	• "Electronic medical records" (EMR) system
A patient must wait at the clinic so that she/he is available when her/his name is called (for consultation/ treatment) so that the SPC's resources are efficiently utilized	• A patient can wait in more pleasant surroundings or do other things while waiting to be called without adversely affecting efficiency	• Establish a paging system to call the patient 15 minutes before appointment — allow patient to go to the cafeteria, book shop, education center, or business center while waiting for main consultation/ treatment
A patient must collect and carry her/his test results with her/him to ensure availability at main consultation	• Test results should be available at main consultation without patient having to carry them along	• All test results scanned in immediately after results are available — no more test results on paper, to be eventually integrated into EMR
HOW Template		
A patient can only be tested by taking a sample or doing a scan, etc.	• A patient can be tested remotely • A patient can conduct the test himself	• Remote diagnostic equipment • Test-kits for self-administered testing

The next step after idea generation is for the team to organize the list into meaningful groups of related ideas, which will eventually become projects. These projects are made of consistent and interdependent ideas built around a central theme. This will allow an individual project to be implemented independent of each other. The following questions are helpful in grouping the ideas together into projects. These questions are intended to guide the staff in grouping projects together.

1. What ideas are similar or seem to be based on the same theme?
   For example, some ideas may be built on outsourcing.
2. In what way is each project different?
   If there is any overlapping of ideas between projects, it may be better to regroup them under different criteria.
3. What about ideas that do not seem to fit anywhere?
   There will always be some ideas that do not fit into any of the projects and it is fine to leave them out.
4. Are there any projects that are related to each other?
   This is discouraged, as the main objective is to allow any project to be implemented individually.

The following projects are proposed for the specialist private clinic.

Create a Health Promotion Agency
• Preventive care program for high-risk groups
• General education on health care projects, costs, etc.

Partner with Private Clinic
• Phone/electronic consultation
• Collect samples/perform simple (preliminary) tests on behalf of the SPC
• Perform presumptive treatment in consultation with the SPC specialist
• Perform follow-up treatment in consultation with the SPC specialist
• Recommend tests in consultation with the SPC specialist (patient can go directly for tests on the first visit, avoiding initial consultation)
• Prescribe/renew medication on advice of the SPC specialist

Optimize the Flow Within the Facility
• General lab combining urine/blood testing and non-invasive cardio testing
• One general lab on each floor (only special equipment labs to be centralized)
• Locate frequently co-occurring tests close together
• Locate labs close to clinics which most frequently order them

Set up a Kiosk for Registration
• Patient registers herself/himself on arrival
• Kiosk prints routing card with shortest/fastest route

Set up a Mobile Clinic
• Equipped with basic test facilities and electronic link to the SPC (transmission of test results)
• Equipped with remote diagnostic equipment for direct, remote examinations by doctor back at the SPC
• Perform treatment in (remote) consultation with doctor at the SPC
• Specially-trained nurses to carry out treatment under (remote) instruction
• Dispense medication

Set up Service Centers Near Patients
• Conveniently located and more accessible than the main SPC
• Basic testing capabilities (may be expanded later)
• Consultation/treatment for some types of disciplines (not requiring heavy testing)
• Prescribing/dispensing medication
• Dispensing diagnostic test-kits

Provide Telemedicine
• Need remote diagnostic equipment (if diagnosis is synchronous)
• Need electronic test result (if diagnosis is asynchronous)

Offer Electronic Medical Records (EMR)
• Complete online availability of all patients' records
• Replaces all paper records pertaining to patients

Provide Mobile Payment
• Direct charge to credit cards (phone authorization)
• Mobile payments and e-wallet

Reorganize Post-Consultation Process
• Combine billing for tests, consultations, treatments, and medication
• Single person to handle payment receipt and appointment booking

Reorganize Pharmacy
• Electronic prescription sent to pharmacy immediately after main consultation
• Pharmacy consolidates medication by clinics
• Delivers medication to clinics (ready for patient to collect after treatment/post-consultation)
• Pharmacy prepares medication for patients to pick up after post-consultation (without waiting)

Allow Patient to Move Around the Premises
• Patients allowed to visit bookshop, cafeteria, and education/business center while waiting for main consultation
• Mobile application to alert patients 15 minutes before consultation

Provide Mobile Applications
• Located in common areas of the SPC
• Provide electronic map for directions
• Provide healthcare information/advice

Once the potential initiatives are identified by the brainstorming team(s), it is time to stack these up against each other and go through a prioritization exercise. This way of arriving at the results based on scoring made by the whole team will make it easier for each member to accept the selected digital initiatives or projects later. It is not necessary that only projects with high scores should be selected. Initiatives that collectively satisfy all benefit criterion to an acceptable degree are much preferred to achieve a win-win situation. Another consideration is to ensure that the selected projects do not interfere with each other negatively and are easy to integrate. For example, the staff avoid selecting one project that involves outsourcing a task and another project that involves building capabilities for the same task. In fact, they should select projects that reinforce each other or are able to achieve economies of scale. Figure 25 illustrates how the evaluation of projects was done for the SPC.

Options	Customer Benefits				Organizational Benefits						Aversion Factors			
	Quality/ Effectiveness	Speed/ Responsiveness	Convenience/ Accessibility	Others	Operational Savings	Productivity /Efficiency	Capacity	Strategic Advantage	Image	Others	Implementation Costs	Difficulty	Risk	Others
GPs/Polyclinics	-	+++	+++			+	++	++	++		-	--	---	
Rearrange SOC		++	+								--	--		
Self-reg. kiosks		++	+		-	+			+		-	--	-	
Travellators		++	+		-				+		--	-		
Service Centre	+	+++	+++		---	+	+++	+++	+++		---	---	---	
Doctors at office	-				--	+	+		-		-	--	--	
EMR	+				+	++	+		+		--	--	-	
ETR		+	+		+	++	+		+		-	--	-	
ES on Web	+	+			-	+	+	+	++		-	-	-	
Reorg. post-consult.		+	+		+						-			
JIT Pharmacy		++	+						+		-	-		
Roaming patients			++		-	-		+	++		-	-	-	
Patient counsellors	++	+	++		--	-		+	+++		-			
Roving test labs		+	++		--	--	-		+		-	-	-	
SOC on wheels	+	+++	+++		---	-	--	++	+++		--	---	---	
Roving pharmacy		+	+		--	-	-				-	--	-	
Pharmacy tie-ups		+	++		-			+	+		-	--	-	

Figure 25. Scoring of each project for the private clinic

The next step is to integrate the selected projects into a new process. This involves developing a "sketch" of how selected projects will be integrated and work together by trial and error. It may require additional ideas or enhancements and information technology (IT) can be considered at this point to improve overall design. An example of how IT can be used in the process includes the following:

- Automation: Can the process be automated to remove human intervention?
- Information: Can the information be captured to better understand the process?
- Sequence: Can the sequence of processes be changed and done concurrently using IT?
- Tracking: Can IT be used to monitor progress of the process?
- Analysis: Can IT be used to analyze information to improve decision-making?
- Geographic: Can IT be used to coordinate processes across distances?
- Integration: Can IT be used to integrate tasks and data?

The new process for a SPC is mapped out after integrating the selected projects, as shown in Figure 26. In the new process, patients can now perform simple testing and diagnostics in a polyclinic before going to a SPC. At the SPC, the patient can pre-register online or register himself at the kiosk and proceed to the test center with the shortest queue. Once the tests are completed, he is free to shop or eat at a nearby shop. 15 minutes before the actual consultation, he will be alerted from the mobile application. After the consultation, he will either receive treatment or go directly to the pharmacy to collect his medication. He will end his visit by paying all his bills in one go and make his next appointment if necessary. The new process was validated to ensure that it is feasible and to solicit a buy-in.

Benefits of Using the New System

- Quick response (QR) codes on mobile phone that are also paperless Environment friendly
- Online pre-registration to schedule or change appointment

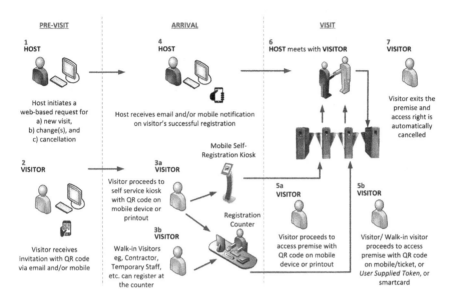

Figure 26.   New process flow for the specialist private clinic

- Quick visitor registration process in the SPC
- Smooth and productive operations derived from real-time integration
- Cost savings from reduced manpower in the SPC

The entire system is to be user friendly and simple to use as most of the patients are quite old in age. Nurses may need to assist them if they are not able to move around easily and the streamline layout helps to minimize movement. The system needs to operate in real-time mode to capture the patient's information from the laboratory results before the doctor can diagnose the patient. The technology used needs to be stable and reliable so that patients and doctors can reply on them. Furthermore, since most of the information about the patient is confidential, patients' records need to be securely stored.

Chapter 9

MANAGING PROCESS CHANGE WITH SUPPLY CHAIN PARTNERS

As we have seen through Chapters 2 to 7, the digital supply chain transformation (DSCT) principles, framework, and methodology have implicit changes in business processes, technology, and the ways of working of staff associated with the supply chain functions undergoing transformation. In this chapter, we will highlight the nuances for managing and ensuring the required change is readily adopted not only within the organization that has embarked on DSCT, but also the supply chain partners. Managing change itself has at least two meanings.

The first meaning of managing change refers to the making of changes in a planned and managed or systematic fashion. The aim is to implement new methods and systems more effectively in an ongoing organization. The changes to be managed lie within the supply chain ecosystem and are controlled by the organization. However, these internal changes might have been triggered by events originating outside the organization(s) participating in DSCT from either their suppliers or customers.

Hence, the second meaning of managing change is the response to changes over which the organization exercises little or no control (e.g. legislation, social and political upheaval, the actions of competitors, national disasters, and so on).

The underlying motive for change management is to make it part of the company culture. However, the culture within the company is frequently underestimated. According to Carly Fiorina, ex-chief executive officer of

Hewlett-Packard, "Culture is the company's software", and "the soft stuff is the hard stuff". Culture is a vital aspect within change management and the crucial factor for success or disaster. Managing the kinds of changes encountered by and instituted within organizations requires a set of comprehensive skills.

Critical Skills for Change Management

Political skills: organizations are, first and foremost, social systems. Without people there can be no organization. Lose sight of this fact and any would-be change agent will likely lose his or her head, especially in Asia's context. Organizations are hotly and intensely political. Change agents dare not join in this game, but they had better understand it. This is one area where you must make your own judgments and keep your own counsel; no one can do it for you.

Analytical skills: make no mistake about it, those who would be change agents had better be very good at something, and that something had better be analysis. Insight is nice, even useful, and sometimes shines with brilliance, but it is difficult to sell and almost impossible to solicit buy-in. A clear, rational, and well-argued process analysis can certainly justify the business process re-engineering efforts and discomfort over the duration. If not, then the political issues have not been adequately addressed. Two particular sets of skills are very important here: (1) work-flow operations or systems analysis and (2) financial analysis.

Change agents must learn to take apart and reassemble operations and systems in novel ways, and then determine the financial and political impacts of what they have done. Conversely, they must be able to start with some financial measure or indicator, or goal, and make their way quickly to those operations and systems that, if reconfigured a certain way, would have the desired financial impact.

People skills: as stated earlier, people are part of an organization. Moreover, they become characterized by all manner of sizes, shapes, colors, intelligence and ability levels, gender, sexual preferences, national origins, first and second languages, religious beliefs, attitudes toward life and work, personalities, and priorities — and these are just a few of the dimensions along which people vary, especially in Asia. We have to deal with them all. The skills most needed in this area are those that typically fall under the heading of communication or interpersonal skills.

To be effective, we must be able to listen actively, restate, reflect, clarify without interrogating, draw out the speaker, lead or channel a discussion, and plant ideas, and develop them. This is especially so in Asia, where most people tend to keep information to themselves and are not keen to share with one another. So, we have to learn to see things through the eyes of these other inhabitants of the organizational world. A situation viewed from a manager's frame of reference is an entirely different situation when seen through the eyes of an operator. Part of the job of a change agent is to reconcile and resolve the conflict between and among disparate (and sometimes desperate) points of view.

Leadership skills: leadership is the act of creating organizational vision, alignment, and deployment. Once the organization is clearly committed to its core vision, a vision specific for the transformation effort should be created. After a process has been chosen for transformation, a vision describing its purpose must be developed. This is critical for focusing the transformation team on its goal. This vision must then be communicated through the entire organization to achieve commitment to the transformation effort and the changes that will ensue.

The responsibility of creating the process vision in most cases falls upon the senior management but can be revised after the more "micro" and complex work of transformation teams has taken place. Therefore, the skill most needed in this case is communicating the process vision to everyone effectively and guiding team members in the right direction to reach the vision.

Leading Change Model

As stated earlier, change happens within supply chain processes due to internal and external factors. As an organization, you have to anticipate quickly and be flexible. Our organizations work the way they do because of how we think and interact. Only by changing how we think can we change deeply-embedded policies and practices. Only by changing how we interact can shared visions, shared understandings, and new capacities for coordinated action be established.

Shared Vision

The practice of shared vision involves the skills of unearthing shared "pictures of the future" that foster genuine commitment and enrollment rather than compliance. The major aspect with change is motivating and educating people and creating a shared vision. It is important for success that this vision is carried by an idea held by your employees. They have to believe that the change is necessary to make it happen! Therefore, we always start with investigating what kind of people we have to manage (awareness) and creating a shared vision with the management team. The process of building a shared vision is done with the supply chain conceptual approach. With this aid, we are able to include every internal and external condition that influences the vision of the organization.

System Thinking

System thinking is a discipline to gain a better view of the situation. It is a framework for seeing interrelationships rather than things, for seeing patterns of change rather than static snapshots. System thinking offers a language that begins by restructuring how we think. Doing obvious things does not produce the obvious, desired outcome. Real leverage lies in understanding dynamic complexity, not detail complexity. System thinking will allow the company to see the whole picture and set the company direction together as part of team learning to achieve its objectives.

Business Development

The ultimate objective is to develop the organization as a whole in the right direction (as stated in the shared vision) and, in this way, increase revenue and margins.

Personal Mastery

Personal mastery is the discipline of continually clarifying and deepening our personal vision, focusing our energies, developing patience, seeing reality objectively, and being able to adopt change.

Mental Models

"Mental models" are deeply ingrained assumptions, generalizations, or even pictures or images that influence how we understand the world and how we take action.

Team Learning

The discipline of team learning starts with "dialogue", the capacity of members in a team to suspend assumptions and enter into a genuine "thinking together". The discipline of dialogue also involves learning how to recognize the patterns of interaction in teams that undermine learning. The patterns of defensiveness are often deeply ingrained in how a team operates. If unrecognized, they undermine learning. If recognized and surfaced creatively, they can actually accelerate learning.

Chapter 10

SUCCESS STORY IN BUSINESS LICENSING TRANSFORMATION

Transforming Business Licensing in Singapore

This case that we have studied involved investigating the implementation of a key public service process and related processes, and system integration issues in business licensing. Starting a business in Singapore used to be a complicated and tedious process. An applicant needed to first register her/his business as a legal entity. Registration alone could cost up to thousands of dollars. The agency in charge would then "advise" the applicant on the "likely" licenses that she/he would need from other agencies to start her/his business.

A license is a permission to do something that otherwise is forbidden. For instance, a childcare center license is needed before anyone is allowed to run a childcare center. A license is therefore a government privilege. It presumes that the activity in question is a privilege, not a right. A license also involves the policing power of the state. That is, if one violates the licensing law, either by acting without a license or failing to uphold the conditions governing the license privilege, one is subjected to prosecution under the civil or criminal laws of the governing body. As such, admittedly or not, licensing is to restrict entry and control a profession or activity.

Class licensing is another form of licensing involving a significant reduction in administration as compared to licensing. Under this regime, conditions are stated upfront so that the applicant can declare that she/he is aware of these conditions of the license and proceed to apply for it.

Agencies can conduct inspections after the license has been issued. If the applicant were found to have breached the conditions, the agencies could then act against her/him. Evidently, the main difference between class licensing as compared to the "conventional" licensing regime is the absence of pre-screening. The conditions that are favorable for implementation of class licensing are as follows:

- There is still a need to actively regulate the business environment because of high costs involved.
- Pre-screening is not necessary and the business activity as a whole is seen to be beneficial to the populace.
- Control as well as meeting of the policy objectives is enforcement-based.
- Extensive information about the business is necessary to enforce licensing rules.

Obtaining or renewing a business-related license in Singapore was a time consuming and complex process until recently. This was especially true for new businesses and others unfamiliar with the licensing process. Even if an applicant had the required knowledge regarding a license application, she/he still had to deal with multiple agencies and repeatedly filling up application forms with the same information, as illustrated in Figure 27. For example, the setting up of a public entertainment outlet required licenses or permits from at least two agencies.

The applicant could confirm her/his business registration or wait for the results of License X and Y before confirming the business registration. Payment signified the applicant's acceptance or confirmation of the approved application. If License X or Y were not approved, she/he could terminate the business registration. If the business registration were not approved, she/he could similarly terminate the license application. The entire process could take up to a few months. In the worst-case scenario, the applicant might be denied a critical license without which she/he could not start the business, despite having forked out a significant amount of time and money for registration and other licenses.

The case of a restaurant start-up in Singapore illustrates this situation: the license application for converting a warehouse into a restaurant was

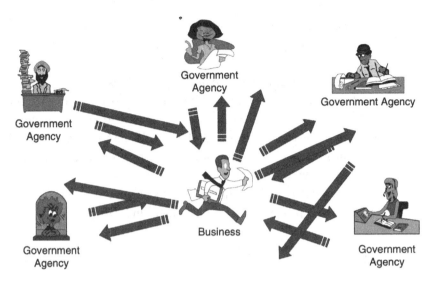

Figure 27. Original business licensing process

approved by one agency and the fee was collected, but the start-up had to be abandoned as another agency later rejected the application because of potential traffic problems.

OASIS: The Transformation Project

The Online Application System for Integrated Services (OASIS) project was started in August 2001 to focus on a particularly important form of red tape for start-ups: *licenses*. This is because start-ups are likely to be most disadvantaged by red tape due to their lack of resources. The project was led by the Ministry of Trade and Industry (MTI) and involved more than 30 other government agencies and their 154 licenses that are relevant for start-ups. The most important and unique element of the OASIS project was the review of rules and licenses related to the setting up of businesses. At least 10% of licenses were committed by agencies for removal, and the average processing time of these licenses was reduced from 3 weeks to 12.5 days.

The targeted customers are start-ups in any sector, as well as existing companies venturing into new sectors. OASIS offers users an online one-stop service to meet their regulatory obligations prior to starting their business. The key value propositions of OASIS include:

- Reducing the inconvenience of manual applications
- Consolidating, integrating, and making various processes transparent
- Allowing the applicant to enter essential information only once to concurrently register the business and apply for multiple licenses and permits (information will automatically be relayed to the backend systems of relevant agencies)
- Making it less costly and much quicker to start up a business
- Fostering a more pro-enterprise environment in Singapore

Vision of OASIS

The vision of OASIS has been to enable its customers to meet the regulatory requirements needed to start a business in a hassle-free manner, entirely through the Internet. While it has defined its niche within the scope of critical regulatory requirements to start a business, OASIS has the potential to be eventually scaled up as a one-stop business center encompassing sales tax registration, employee retirement fund registration, etc.

OASIS Project Team

The OASIS team comprised of a high-level steering committee (SC), the core team, and the authorized agency officers (AAOs). The OASIS SC, chaired by the Deputy Secretary of MTI and co-chaired by the Deputy Secretary of the Ministry of Finance (MOF), consists of representatives from the key ministries with license and permit activities. The OASIS SC provides a channel to surface issues for higher-level decisions. The OASIS SC meets once every month, but should expedited resolutions be needed, discussions and decisions are done through electronic means. The core team, comprising MTI and Infocomm Media Development Authority (IMDA) officers, plays the role of co-coordinator and facilitator to help ensure that all aspects of the project are competently executed. The core team reports to the SC on the status of the project and seeks directions on

Table 13. Project phases for the OASIS transformation

Phase 1	Phase 2	Phase 3	Phase 4
Review licensing process	Challenge assumptions and generate ideas	Apply redesign principles	Implement new process

difficult issues. The AAOs are appointed by their respective licensing agencies to maintain their license content in the OASIS website, ensuring that license information and business rules are promptly and accurately created and updated.

The transformation project requirements were broad, covering many agencies and licenses, and spread over a number of years. The total cost, estimated at between US$3.5 million and US$5 million, was funded by MOF. The size, complexity, and cost of the project warranted a phased approach to mitigate inherent risks and benefit from progressive experience and learning while engaging the various stakeholders when and where they were needed. Key activities were also defined for the various phases to direct and control the project (see Table 13). While MTI and IMDA committed its officers to manage the project, the respective agencies provided the necessary manpower and information technology (IT) professionals to implement the necessary changes on their end and to ensure system compatibility with OASIS.

Phase 1: Review Licensing Process

This initial phase involved an extensive government-wide review of agency licenses to validate the need for the license. Furthermore, it included a review of compliance cost and licensing fees for businesses and an examination of flexible licensing systems. The team's initial efforts in getting agencies to review their licensing policies encountered some difficulties:

- Agencies have little incentive or motivation to get rid of a license, particularly if revenues are collected from the issuance of the license.
- Agencies are concerned that without the license, effective regulation or enforcement cannot be assured, thus compromising safety and quality standards.

- Agencies cite some "difficulties" in revoking licenses.
- There may be hidden or additional requirements that are not so apparent on paper.

However, these statements tend to be indicative of general inertia and resistance to change, particularly since many agencies may feel that an existing system is already working well (at least, for administrative convenience) and generating substantial revenue. Furthermore, there is a tendency toward being agency-centric in carrying out a regulatory function as opposed to being customer-centric.

To change the mindset of these agencies, a broad principle was recommended by the OASIS SC in rethinking current policies toward customer-centricity: process re-engineering focusing on customer-centricity, yet tempered with the basic regulatory needs. Minimal regulatory costs in terms of time and money expended should be imposed on the customer in order to fulfil the regulatory requirements. Government agencies have to put business customers first and plan the processes around their needs, looking at innovative and cost-effective solutions. These agencies must adopt a mindset that the licensing system is to be customer-centric and pro-enterprise while meeting regulatory requirements. This approach is a sheer contrast from the previous approach where delivery of the licensing services was organized along agencies' silo regulatory processes, leading to cumbersome and costly red tape for businesses. At the same time, various requirements and processes should be made as transparent as possible.

Phase 2: Challenge Assumptions and Generate Ideas

The review of existing licensing regulations and policies required agencies to re-examine various facets of the licensing regime through a series of questions, enabling agencies to challenge assumptions they had taken for granted:

- What is the rationale of the license?
- What is the fee charged to the applicant?

- What was the initial cost incurred by the agency for the purpose of administering the regulation?
- What is the cost incurred by the agency for each additional applicant?
- What are the requirements for approval of this license?
- Are these requirements waived occasionally? If so, how often?
- Do you usually need to have applicants meet with your agency to provide additional information face to face?
- Is there a regulatory check before the license is issued?
- How often is the application rejected and usually for what reasons?
- How often is enforcement conducted after the license is issued?
- How often have offenders been caught in violation of the rules?

Phase 3: Apply Redesign Principles

It is pertinent that the license process is redesigned to align with key business objectives. The core team recommended the following key redesign principles for the new license process:

Principle 1. Organize work around outcomes, not tasks

The idea of e-enabling the license application process is to bring added convenience to businesses. It is therefore important that the process is not merely one that transfers bureaucracy online. With OASIS, the applicant only needs to log-on once to apply for several approvals in one session. If the applicant chooses to apply for more than one license, all relevant data fields pertaining to each license will be pulled together into a single set of forms so that the applicant can apply for the various approvals in a single form-filling process.

Principle 2. Let those who use the process perform the process

The Online Business License Profiler generates a list of licenses for the applicant based on her/his desired business activity using rule-based technology, allowing her/him to select the licenses to be applied for. The applicant can also search for licenses from the listing of government agencies or by using the search engine.

Principle 3. Capture information once — at the source

With the integrated form, common information will be filled in only once. Data housed within common government databases will be utilized to populate fields asking for standard information. Where the information requested is common across agencies, the data labels will be standardized where possible (for example, manager, key executive, authorized person, contact person, etc.). The applicant will be updated of changes to the application status through e-mail and/or short message service (SMS) alerts. Alternatively, the applicant can check the status of all transactions online on the OASIS website.

Principle 4. Put the decision point where the work is performed and build control in the process

Instead of signing and declaring the authenticity of information multiple times, OASIS allows the applicant to make an electronic declaration just once. This single declaration will be accepted by all agencies involved.

Principle 5. Link or convert sequential activities into parallel activities

All agencies involved will concurrently receive the same transaction information. The agencies will know which other licenses the applicant is concurrently applying for and the results of the relevant applications. Such information allows parallel processing by agencies and allows dependencies to be coordinated through OASIS. As OASIS works toward shortening the entire process of starting up, agencies need to adhere to certain levels of service standards, thus ensuring that the applications are processed in a timely fashion.

Principle 6. Look for ways to postpone the final product

At any point in time, the applicant has the flexibility to terminate applications and accept approved applications. For example, should the applicant wish to register the business first with the approved licenses for her/his main activity while waiting for some other license approvals, he is able to do so. On the other hand, in the event that the license is not approved, the applicant can terminate his business registration (within a 14-day window).

Principle 7. Avoid duplicating task with supply chain members

The applicant is able to pay for all her/his license and processing fees through a consolidated payment. All funds would be paid into a central account before being disbursed to the appropriate agencies.

Phase 4: Implement the New Process

During implementation, internal approval processes for licenses need to be redesigned by each agency and streamlined to allow businesses to obtain approvals quickly. Standardization of forms and utilizing the strategic application of information and communications technology (ICT) for integration and concurrent processing are needed to bring about time and costs saving for businesses. The following steps briefly describe the new business licensing process of OASIS (shown in Figure 28) and how it interacts with the respective government agencies involved.

1. The applicant needs to log-on to the online system to apply for one or more licenses to get the respective agency approvals in a single sign-on session.
2. The applicant needs to complete an integrated standardized form with common information from common government databases populating fields asking for standard information.
3. Upon completing data entry, the applicant will make an electronic declaration just once, which is accepted by all government agencies involved.
4. The submitted transaction information from the applicant will be concurrently received by agencies involved in approving the relevance business license(s).
5. Once an agency approves (or rejects) an application, an e-mail and/or an SMS will be automatically sent to inform the applicant.

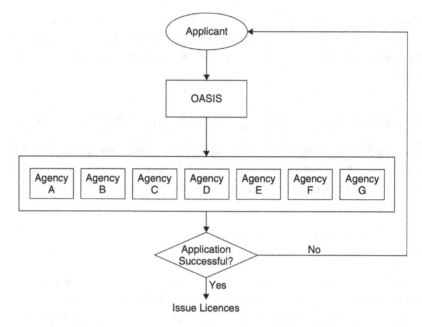

Figure 28. The new business licensing process

The applicant whose license(s) has been approved can then make a consolidated payment through the system.

The OASIS transformation project resulted in the development and delivery of the OASIS portal to allow businesses to apply for licenses needed to start their businesses without resorting to over-the-counter (offline) means. The OASIS portal is part of the whole government solution to create a more pro-enterprise environment in Singapore, particularly for new entrepreneurs who do not have the resources and expertise to navigate the current licensing systems.

Project Outcomes from OASIS

The following is a summary of key benefits realized from the implementation of the OASIS portal gathered by the transformation core team (MTI, Singapore, 2007):

- *24 by 7 one-stop shop for licenses*: The OASIS portal provides a one-stop licensing shop ("many agencies, one government") which is convenient for business users to apply for new licenses and update/renew/terminate existing licenses, and provides a consolidated payment mechanism. The applicant would only need to complete one integrated form for multiple licenses and make a one-time payment. Previously, applicants would need to complete one form after another at different government agencies, often providing the same information and making separate payments.

- *Removal of irrelevant and obsolete licenses*: More than 260 licenses were reviewed. In all, about 10% of start-up licenses were removed or merged with other licenses or converted into once-off lifetime licenses to reduce compliance costs and burden to businesses. Examples of irrelevant licenses include the Hatchery and Stable Licenses and the license for private parking space.
- *Faster application and processing time*: Since business license application processes were simplified, the average processing time for licenses was reduced from 21 days to 8 days, allowing applicants to obtain the necessary approvals earlier, as shown in Table 14. Applicants also experienced a reduction in the average time spent to apply for licenses from five hours to one hour or less.

Table 14. Benefits to the applicants and agency after the transformation

Licenses	Over-The-Counter	Online (OASIS Portal)
Incorporate a new company	Cost: US$720 to US$12,600 depending on company size Processing time: 5 days	Cost: Flat fee of US$180 Processing time: 2 hours
Application for change of use (Urban Redevelopment Authority)	Cost: US$720	Cost: US$480
Application for swimming pool license	Renew license annually	One-off lifetime registration (No need for renewal)
Application for pet shop license	Processing time: 2 months	Processing time: 3 days
Application for food shop license	Photocopy of company business profile, floor plan, and fire safety certificate as supporting documents	No need for these documents during application process

Managing cross-agency or supply chain projects for online e-services has never been easy. The OASIS project has provided valuable insights into how business licenses can be re-engineered in an effective manner, notwithstanding the challenges faced when integrating information from multiple agencies.

Organizational challenges refer to working in silos as opposed to working in a team; culture challenges refer to a mindset change from a regulatory perspective to a customer-centric view. This shift will require a high level of process harmonization and systems interoperability between different internal functions and external organizations to enable better online, real-time communication and information exchange. While this research has identified one example of process inefficiencies for one of the business processes, we can argue that there will be many other inefficient processes existing as well. Therefore, to realize more customer-focused service delivery in the country, public sector agencies will require a substantial level of integration of backend information systems such as tax systems, retirement systems, company registers, and land and property systems. According to one of the directors from MTI who manages the OASIS portal, it is important to maintain the balance between the need to regulate the activities and the interests of businesses. The team adopted a system-thinking approach, conducting regular focus group sessions with businesses to obtain feedback on their start-up experiences. Such feedback sessions drove the team to constantly seek ways to improve the design and features of the OASIS portal.

In order to overcome these challenges when integrating processes from multiple agencies, it requires policy reviews, business process re-engineering, and system changes. These changes will not happen without top management being seen championing them, thus sending a positive signal to agency staff to dedicate themselves to the success of OASIS. The team had to manage concerns faced by individual agencies to secure buy-in and commitment from agencies. The team learned to recognize, acknowledge, and manage specific concerns of agencies through regular consultations and meeting sessions held with agencies. It is therefore important to secure commitment from senior management of agencies from the outset to ensure smoother implementation. Top management support will assist to allocate appropriate resources and to resolve conflicting priorities. Therefore, it is understandable that for the public sector, these changes will be even more severe in an environment that can be described as bureaucratic, functionally oriented, and a legacy system.

Lack of synergy among different government agencies and private agencies' business processes proves that much more needs to be done in terms of fundamentally rethinking and radically re-engineering these processes if joint services are to be delivered through a single point of access. The OASIS team learned the importance of having in place a mechanism to refer unresolved matters to higher authorities. In cases where problems or issues cannot be resolved at the working level, the team escalates the issue to committees that are chaired by senior civil service leaders. Agencies would generally try to resolve issues without the intervention of these high-level committees.

As the implementation of these licenses in OASIS involves in excess of 20 agencies, close cooperation and coordination is vital. Agencies would have to closely adhere to the schedules drawn up in order for the licenses to be implemented in a timely fashion. From an organizational perspective, the paradigm shift that needs to be realized to change these processes would mean that the government will need to breakdown their departmental or silo culture and overcome resistance to change, as seen in other forms of organizational change such as business process re-engineering.

Lastly, the website for this project is now online at https://www.bizfile.gov.sg/ and it is managed by the Accounting and Corporate Regulatory Authority (ACRA), which is the regulator of business registration, financial reporting, public accountants, and corporate service providers.

Chapter 11

CRITERIA FOR SUCCESS IN DIGITAL SUPPLY CHAIN TRANSFORMATION

Finally, we would like to discuss key elements of success in driving towards a digital supply chain transformation. Critical success factors remain within the control of the program manager who is responsible for implementing the digital supply chain transformation project. Rather than being held captive to a chain of events beyond their control, program managers have a strong capacity to influence and improve their teams' chances of implementation success by attending to the critical success factors as listed below.

Project Goals and Mission

Goals, as well as the ultimate benefits, must be clearly defined at the outset of a digital supply chain transformation project. Project mission refers to a condition where the goals of the project are clear and understood not only by the project team involved, but also by the other organizations in the supply chain.

Top Management Commitment

Obtaining stakeholders commitment: top management or sponsors from each company must set the stage for both the design project and subsequent implementation.

Top management commitment refers to the willingness of top management and supply chain leaders to provide the necessary resources and authority or power for implementation success. Management commitment for digital supply chain transformation projects, or indeed for any implementation effort, has been considered of great importance in distinguishing between their ultimate success and failure. The degree of management support for a digital supply chain transformation project will lead to significant variations in the degree of acceptance or resistance to that project or product. Top management's support of such project may involve aspects such as allocation of sufficient resources (including financial, manpower, time, etc.) as well as the project management's confidence in their support in the event of crisis.

Detailed Schedule

A detailed schedule or plan is a detailed specification of the individual action steps for digital technologies implementation. Project schedule must be driven by the importance of creating a detailed plan of the required stages in the digital transformation process. Schedule or plan refers to the degree to which time schedules, milestones, manpower, and equipment requirements are specified. The schedule should include a satisfactory measurement system as a way of judging actual performance against budget and time allowances. Schedules and plans are not the same. Planning is a more broad-range process, encompassing resource assessments, work breakdown structures, and other forms of project monitoring mechanisms. Scheduling is generally understood to refer to the tasks of creating specific time and task-interdependent structures, such as critical path and Gantt charts.

Stakeholder Feedback

Stakeholder feedback is the communication, consultation, and active listening to all parties impacted by the proposed digital supply chain transformation project. A stakeholder is anyone who will ultimately make use of the results of the project either as a customer or supplier outside the company. The degree to which stakeholders are personally involved in the implementation process will lead to great variation in their support for that project. Hence, the program manager must determine whether stakeholders for the project have been identified, onboarded, continuously updated, and their needs met.

Talent Management

Talent management includes recruitment, selection, and training of the necessary personnel for the program implementation team. In many situations, personnel chosen for the digital supply chain transformation project team have inadequate skills necessary to actively contribute to implementation success. One research study has defined "people" as a situational variable whose knowledge, skills, goals, and personalities must be considered in assessing the environment of the organization for successful project implementation. Hence, personnel, as a factor, is concerned with developing an implementation team with the requisite skills and commitment to perform their function.

Technical Feasibility for Digitalization

Technical feasibility is the availability of technology and expertise to accomplish the specific technical action steps to bring each digitalization project "live". The team refers to the need of ensuring that the necessary personnel of the implementation team possess the required digital technology skills and have adequate technology infrastructure to perform their tasks. The decision to initiate a new digital supply chain transformation project must be affirmed on the organization's ability to both staff the team with competent individuals and provide the technical means for the project to succeed.

Supply Chain Partner Buy-in

Supply chain partner buy-in is the selling of the final process to its ultimate intended users. It refers to the final stage in the implementation process, at which time the overall usefulness and worth of the digital supply chain transformation project is to be determined. Some researchers even proposed the use of intermediaries to act as a liaison between the designer, or implementation team, and the project's potential users to aid in client acceptance. The sequence of operations concerned with the client follows this pattern:

- Consult to determine specific needs
- Sell the ideas (including the benefits of the project), budgets, and time frame for completion
- Perform a final verification of client acceptance once the project has been completed

The verification may be in the form of a series of formal interviews or follow-up conversations with clients who are intending to use the process.

Monitoring and Feedback

Monitoring and feedback refers to the timely provision of comprehensive control information at each stage in the implementation process. It is the control process at each stage of the digital supply chain transformation project implementation where key personnel receive feedback on how the project is comparing to initial projections. Making allowances for adequate monitoring and feedback mechanisms gives the program manager the ability to anticipate problems, oversee corrective measures, and ensure that no deficiencies are overlooked. Program managers need to emphasize the importance of constant monitoring and fine-tuning implementation. Hence, monitoring and feedback refers not only to the project schedule and budget, but also monitoring performance of members of the project schedule and budget, as well as the project team.

Communication

Communication refers to the provision of an appropriate network and necessary information dissemination to all key actors in the project implementation process. The need for adequate communication channels is extremely important in creating an atmosphere for successful digital supply chain transformation implementation. Communication is not only essential within the project team itself, but also between the team and both the rest of the organization and the external supply chain. Hence, the feedback mechanism is a necessity for exchanging information with external supply chain partners and the rest of the organization concerning the project's capabilities, the goals of the implementation process, the changes in policies and procedures, the status reports, and so on.

Troubleshooting

Troubleshooting is the ability to handle unexpected crises and deviations from the plan. Problem areas exist in every digital supply chain transformation. The measure of a successful project implementation effort is not the avoidance of problems but knowing the correct steps to take once problems develop. The program manager should make adequate initial arrangements for troubleshooting mechanisms to be included in the implementation plan. Such mechanisms would make it easier not only to react to problems as they arise, but also to foresee and possibly forestall potential problem areas in the implementation process.

Chapter 12

SUCCESS STORY IN DIGITAL SUPPLY CHAIN TRANSFORMATION

In Chapter 8, we discussed a case study with an excellent example of processes assessment that established the foundation for transformation. In the same chapter, we also read about the specialist clinic which went on a very exhaustive path of comprehensive process redesign that led into the technology transformation stage. In Chapter 10, we saw an end-to end transformation case study which started with process analysis and redesign through to a digital platform implementation. Finally, we provide here a complete case study which leverages on futuristic digital levers while starting with a solid foundation of business process transformation of the supply chain.

Case Study: Transforming the Less than Container Load (LCL) Business using Blockchain and Internet of Things

Founded in 1987, Belgium, ECU Worldwide (ECU) is a global leader in non-vessel operating common carrier services. Backed by a rich legacy, passion, and agility, the company has brought in world-class innovations in LCL and set several benchmarks in the industry over the last two decades.

Allcargo Logistics Ltd., India's largest integrated logistics solutions provider in the private sector, acquired the company in 2006, which resulted in further efficiency improvements in operations. In May 2016, the company was rebranded as ECU Worldwide and consolidated their global presence by bringing all the offices under a single name to denote well-knit offices and highly-coordinated operations. The quest to bring geographies closer to their customers has remained unchanged, thus etching the philosophy of 'Geography Simplified'.

As more countries are industrializing and manufacturing sectors are expanding their businesses, they would normally outsource their logistics requirements to be handled by third-party logistics providers. Therefore, the expected demand in the logistics sector would be expected to grow as countries were able to maintain an average growth of seven to eight percent annually.

Led by a strong management team, and offices in 160 countries, the company is now offering LCL and FCL (full container load) services across the globe. Its wide variety of value-added services and logistics solutions make them excel in handling and transporting complex cargo to anywhere in the world in a seamless way.

Mission of ECU Worldwide

To simplify geographies with the expertise of their human resources through seamless integration of their offices and world-class technology.

Vision of ECU Worldwide

The vision for the company is "To be the global leader in our business, through customer delight by innovations, agility and sustainable business model." Uday Shetty, the Regional Chief Executive Officer (CEO) for APAC, described that ECU had grown from a small small and medium-sized enterprise to be one of most reputed LCL providers in the world over the past 30 years. As a result of forward integration, ECU had evolved from LCL business to also venture into related industries in the logistics area, such as transportation, warehousing, and distribution.

Presently, ECU's head office is based in Mumbai, India, as explained by Shetty. However, its online system can be accessible anywhere in the world to provide booking and tracking services for their customers.

Over the years in the business, ECU has invested heavily in software to upgrade its systems to meet customers' growing demands for visibility and ease of doing business. "We are glad to share that the entire network is on same IT platform, which makes the operations more uniform and also offers customers similar experiences in service across the world," as commented by Shetty.

Nature of the LCL Business

Shetty explained in detail the logistics industry. He observed that competition in this industry is extremely high, and the business is quite fragmented. The market can be broadly segmented into local forwarder and global forwarders (such as Dalsey, Hillblom and Lynn International GmbH (DHL), Kuehne + Nagel International AG (K&N), DB Schenker , etc.).

The LCL business modus operandi is quite different from the FCL business. While FCL operations and costing are done based on demand and supply, LCL business costing is subjected to the client's requirement. For instance, if clients prefer to have lower ocean freight and higher destination charges, an arrangement can be done accordingly.

Hence the market is segmented into local forwarder and global forwarder business. While local forwarders focus on business, where customers require the lowest possible freight rates (even rebates) and higher destination charges (destination lading charges (DLC)), global forwarders have a balanced approach to keep DLC lower so that consignees are not upset and transactions are hassle-free.

Consolidation operators or competition for ECU is also segmented into local players or regional operators and global players. Local or regional operators mainly focus on the business from smaller forwarders, while global players work with large multinational corporations such as DHL, K&N, and others.

ECU has a fair share of business from both local and global forwarders. Global consolidators have an advantage over smaller operators given the former's network strength (coverage, single identity), visibility, and reliability, but on the other hand, they are faced with niche operators who can offer extremely low rates, given their low-cost operations.

Company Structure

Figure 29 shows ECU's organization structure. The chief executive officer of the Asia-Pacific (APAC) region is headed by Mr. Uday

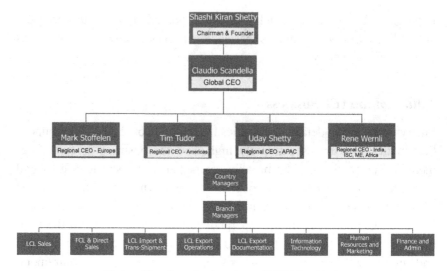

Figure 29. Organization chart of ECU Worldwide

Kumar Shetty, and each Country Manager reports to the Regional Heads (Southeast Asia and North Asia). At the country level, ECU has Branch Managers and Product Managers (for FCL and LCL), and they have dotted line reporting to the Regional Product Heads, who are responsible for strategies development and business development for their regions.

The two main departments in a forwarding business are the import and export departments, while other supporting functions such as Finance, Human Resource, Administration, and Information Technology help to ensure smooth operations.

Import department

The import operations team is responsible for two products: LCL and FCL. For LCL operations, the team has the following responsibilities:

1. Receiving the pre-alert documents of the expected consolidation container
2. Checking the document for correctness, and, in case of any discrepancy, coordinate with the origin office to correct the documents timely

to avoid any customs penalty and inconvenience to the customers at destinations

3. Filing of customs manifest either directly on the customs system or through a third-party vendor

4. Issuing cargo arrival notices to consignees so that they can file the import declaration timely with the customs for clearance of their goods

5. Coordinating with the Container Freight Station (CFS) and carrier for collection of documents, cargo release, arranging devanning of containers, and returning empty container back to the carriers

6. Invoicing customers and closure of file, as per the internal key performance indicators

The process for the FCL import team is similar to LCL import, except that for FCL customers, they have the choice to receive the container at their factory premises to carry out devanning and return the empty container to the carrier yard once they have devanned the cargo contents, as shown in Figure 30.

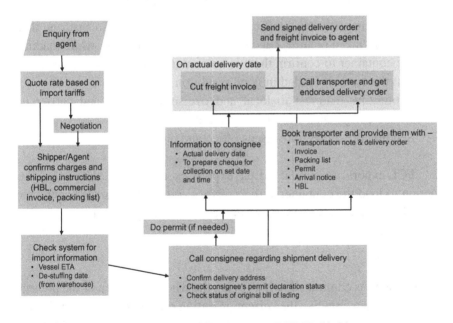

Figure 30.   Import LCL Process at ECU Worldwide

Export department

LCL export operations have a greater workload as compared to imports. For LCL export operations, the team has the following responsibilities:

1. Preparing the export tariff rate card and sharing with the sales department before updating the system
2. Creating the sailing schedule in the system and share with customers on request
3. Receiving bookings from customers and, depending on the cargo receiving date, assigning the shipment to a particular sailing date and providing the booking to customers accordingly
4. Coordinating with the carrier and customer or customer-appointed customs broker to

   a. Follow up on booking confirmation
   b. Confirm cargo receipt with CFS
   c. Arrange 20-feet or 40-feet container(s) based on the total volume
   d. Place booking with carriers
   e. Coordinate with carrier for empty pick up from carrier yard

5. Completing vanning (stuffing) of the container and also ensuring that CFS has taken pictures outside and inside the container while loading the container to confirm there is no container damage and to confirm that the cargo is loaded in good condition at the origin
6. Submitting manifest to local and overseas customs and carrier to ensure compliance with the regulation
7. Sending pre-alerts to overseas office and closing the file

FCL exports are similar to LCL exports except that the shipper has the option to load the container at their factory and send the loaded container straight to the port for vessel loading, as shown in Figure 31.

The Future

Uday Shetty is committed to improving the whole operation of the present company. He would like the current operating procedures to be redesigned such that it is more customer-centric with the help of a new information

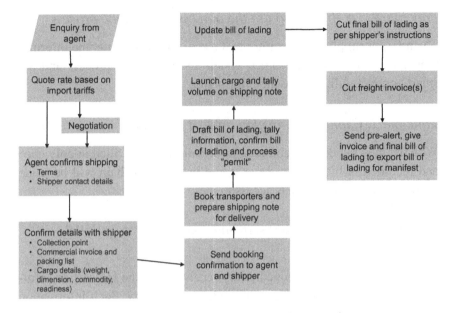

Figure 31. Export LCL process at ECU Worldwide

system for the company. He is keen to use blockchain with Internet of things (IoT) to transform the LCL industry.

Proposed Framework for LCL Business

Based on the requirements from ECU Worldwide, a new framework is proposed based on the following principles and is recommended for any exporters, importers, carriers, and related parties in the seaborne commerce that use containers to transport cargo.

Principle 1. Organize work around outcomes, not tasks

The idea of using blockchain is to bring added convenience to businesses. It is therefore important that the process is not merely one that transfers data online. Users would be able to enter information and blockchain will help store information on a common cloud server as encrypted records.

Principle 2. Let those who use the process perform the process

The relevant supply chain partner in the ecosystem can enter the information into the blockchain-enabled system as part of the process and the smart contract will validate the information.

Principle 3. Capture information once at the source

With the integrated form, common information will be filled in only once and recorded in blockchain. Data stored in the blockchain will be made available to anyone who has access to these data.

Principle 4. Link or convert sequential activities into parallel activities

All parties involved will concurrently receive the same transaction information with blockchain-distributed ledger technology. Such information allows parallel processing by each party and allows dependencies to be coordinated through the system, thus ensuring that applications are processed in a timely fashion.

The proposed framework in Figure 32 shows how blockchain and IoT can cooperate with each other. Generally, IoT technology will help to

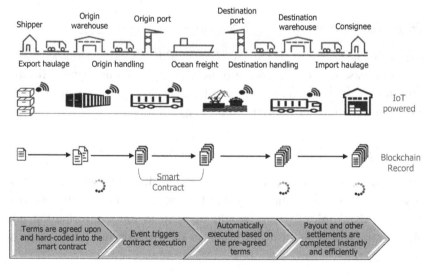

Figure 32. Framework of implementing blockchain and IoT LCL business

track the movement of the container at all times. When it reaches a certain point, blockchain will record and update the activities and information in one integrated system. There will be only one fully integrated logistics ecosystem based on the blockchain. All documents and information, either public or private such as invoices, bills of lading, customs documentation, license, and data sheets, will be stored in the blockchain for all parties to access without the need for a human coordinator to tackle or generate the document. In addition to the above framework, the full shipping information in the form of documents in the process from exporting a cargo from a country to importing that cargo in another country will be shown clearly in real time to the relevant authorized person in the value chain. Figure 33 depicts the various types of documents needed to be transferred according to the cargo when shipping over sea. By using blockchain and IoT, manual processes for all supply chain and trading partners will be minimized by leveraging the paperless trade blockchain network.

Potential Benefits for ECU Worldwide in using the New Platform

Generally, when applying the convergence of IoT and blockchain system, there will be potential benefits in the entire ecosystem besides authenticity assurance. In another words, it is the improvements in each process of the supply chain that help every party strictly control the quality and status of their cargo on the journey transported by container, as shown in Table 15.

In terms of the entities involved in a container shipment, great benefits are accrued to each participant by implementing a new framework. Besides the fact that each party is only concerned about the authenticity of cargo they want to export, there are other overall benefits that they will also perceive in this new advanced configuration.

Potential Risks and Challenges in using the New Platform

It is true that this platform has great merits for connecting every party related to the container conveyance, from seller, buyer, port authorities, carrier, shipper, etc. This framework also provides improvement since most of the previous ones were designed based on a centralized framework. However, there are some challenges and risks with this new conver-

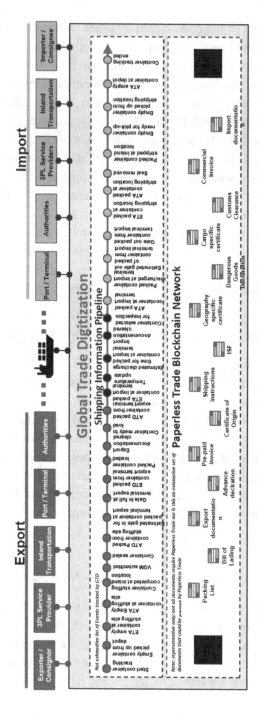

Figure 33. Detailed documentation in global trade digitization and the paperless trade blockchain network

Table 15.   Benefits of IoT and blockchain for all the stakeholders

Procedure	Original	Implementing Blockchain and IoT
Intermodal transport	Issues related to delay, low-quality vehicle, and unlicensed logistics provider. Causing risks to cargo quality.	Provide operational planning and control of the transport network. For example, get access to the distributed system to know information on the disposition of shipments carried on trucks, rail, barges, etc. Personal digital assistant helps drivers get notifications immediately when the containers are available for pick up. In case disruptions occur, all parties will be notified, and decisions and actions can be expedited quickly to minimize the impact of the disruption (reschedule the pick-up and delivery of container)
Loading/ Unloading	Labor workers have to perform loading operations manually, which took many hours to complete. The cargo is also not fully assured to be untouched and secure.	Use IoT devices to track the movement and location of the containers and store this information in the blockchain database. Any abnormal event will be triggered, and a notification will be sent to the relevant parties immediately. This helps to enhance yard operations and save time.
Information transfer	The information from different actors in the journey may be inconsistent. Moreover, it takes more time to transfer information from one party to other. This results in the wasting of time in core container movement.	The information is transmitted constantly and easily across all trade partners. Hence, the container is quickly and accurately dispatched from shipper to the final consignee.
Port and terminal service	Long lead time and lack of coordination in organizing the container.	Provide information about disposition of shipment along with a network of smart sensors, actuators, and wireless devices. Data centers make up the key infrastructure of the smart port, which allow the port authorities to provide essential services in a faster and more efficient manner.

gence of blockchain and IoT. Blockchain alone contains many difficulties in executing and operating the system. The current lack of knowledge of ECU staff to plan, execute, and maintain the new system, which is a combination of blockchain and IoT, will have its own learning curve lead time. Moreover, the full adoption of integrated systems still lacks standards and interoperability. Security is always a concern in implementing any open and sharing platform. The more complicated the platform is, the more easily it can be attacked. Along with the advancement of new technology, attackers can find gaps and cause threats to the system.

APPENDICES

The Business Model Canvas

Team or Company Name: Current Domestic Market

Date: 12 June 2017

[X] Primary Canvas
[ ] Alternative Canvas

Key Partners
- Landlords
- Banks
- Timber suppliers
- Certifying agents

Key Activities
- Leadership
- Marketing
- R&D
- PF production and application

Key Resources
- Veneer supply
- Production plant
- ERP/BI

Value Proposition
- Brand
- Cost performance
- Supply capability
- Reliability
- Lead time
- Innovation

Customer Relationships
- Website
- Sales Representatives

Channels
- Distributor
- Construction Material outlets

Customer Segments
- Project – Commercial Builders
- Retail – House Builder

Cost Structure
- Economics of scales
- Third-party costs
- High fixed costs
- Raw material costs (70%)
- Factory rental
- Labour turnover
- Short cash conversion cycle

Revenue Streams
- Product sales

Appendix 1. Business canvas for current business

The Business Model Canvas

Team or Company Name: New Furniture Market		Date: 12 June 2017		☒ Primary Canvas ☐ Alternative Canvas

Key Partners	Key Activities	Value Proposition	Customer Relationships	Customer Segments
• Bank • Timber suppliers	• R&D • Quality control • Marketing • Procurement • Product Postponement	• High quality • Standard compliance • Supply capacity • Vietnam origin • Consistent quality • Competitive pricing • Wide choice of product range • Extra service added • Human and environment safe • Product performance • Supply capacity • Reasonable price	• Designer • Dedicated sales representatives • Exhibition	• Export Furniture Company • Flooring Producers • Local Furniture Company • Carpenter Workshop
	Key Resources		**Channels**	
	• Veneer supply • Machines • ERP/BI • Market intelligence		• Direct sales • Distributor • Wood product outlet	

Cost Structure	Revenue Streams
• Factory rental • Defective products • Certification and compliance costs • High fixed cost • Economics of scale • Marketing costs • R&D costs	• Product sales

Appendix 2.   Business canvas for future business

Appendix 3. Core team for transformation

GLOSSARY

Artificial intelligence is the branch of computer science that deals with the creation of machines or systems capable of performing functions that would normally require human intelligence. These machines interact with the environment and behave according to the information they receive about it without any human intervention.

A **blockchain** is, in the simplest of terms, a time-stamped series of immutable records of data that is managed by a cluster of computers not owned by any single entity. Each of these blocks of data (i.e. block) is secured and bound to each other using cryptographic principles (i.e. chain).

A **chatbot** is a software application that uses artificial intelligence natural language processing capabilities to converse with customers, usually through a chat program. Such conversations may appear convincingly real that you may not realize you are conversing with a machine and not with another person.

Cloud computing is the delivery of on-demand computing services — from applications to storage and processing power — typically over the Internet and on a pay-as-you-go basis. One benefit of using cloud computing services is that firms can avoid the upfront cost and complexity of owning and maintaining their own information technology infrastructure, and instead simply pay for what they use, when they use it.

A **decision support system (DSS)** is a computerized program used to support determinations, judgments, and courses of action in an organization or a business. A DSS sifts through and analyzes massive amounts of data, compiling comprehensive information that can be used to solve problems and in decision making.

The **Internet of things** (IoT) is a system that connects any electronic device, gadget, machine, microchip, sensor, appliance, building — anything — to the Internet. As a result, all these things can collect information and then share it with each other. Such interconnection of devices and machines allows people to monitor, control, and improve the overall environment.

Robotics is the interdisciplinary technology that combines artificial intelligence and engineering to conceive, build, and operate machines with various purposes.

A **sensor** is an electronic device that measures and monitors environmental conditions. The data recorded by these devices is usually collected by a computer, which then uses the information to take action. Sensors measure physical qualities such as speed and are built into many devices that you use regularly.

Social media is any digital tool that allows users to quickly create and share content with the public. Social media encompasses a wide range of websites and applications. For example, Twitter specializes in sharing links and short written messages.

BIBLIOGRAPHY

Andersen, B. (2007). *Business Process Improvement Toolbox (2nd ed.)*. Milwaukee, WI: ASQ Quality Press.

Attong, M. and Metz, T. (2013). *Change or Die: The Business Process Improvement Manual*. Boca Raton, FL: CRC Press.

Bounfour, A. (2016). *Digital Futures Digital Transformation*. New Yok: Springer.

Brown, T. (2009). *Change by Design: How Design Thinking Transforms Organizations and Inspires Innovation*. New York: HarperCollins Publishers.

Champy, J. (1995). *Reengineering Management: The Mandate for New Leadership*. New York: Harper Business.

Champy, J. and Greenspun, H. (2010). *Reengineering Health Care: A Manifesto for Radically Rethinking Health Care Delivery*. Upper Saddle River, NJ: Pearson.

Chanchaichujit, J., Tan, A., and Meng, F. (2019). *Transforming Healthcare Using Emerging Technologies*. Sage Publications.

Di Martinelly, C., Guinet, A., and Riane, F. (2010). *Reengineering the Hospital Supply Chain: A Methodological Approach Applied to A Case Study*. Saarbrücken, Germany: VDM Verlag Dr. Müller.

Dumas, M., La Rosa, M., Mendling, J., and Reijers, H. A. (2013). *Fundamentals of Business Process Management*. New York: Springer.

Fischer, B., Lago, U., and Liu, F. (2013). *Reinventing Giants: How Chinese Global Competitor Haier has Changed the Way Big Companies Transform*. San Francisco, CA: Jossey-Bass.

Fitzgerald, M., Kruschwitz, N., Bonnet, D., and Welch, M. (2014). Embracing Digital Technology: A New Strategic Imperative. *MIT Sloan Management Review*, 55(2), 1–12.

Hammer, M. (1994). Re-engineering is not Hocus-Pocus. *Across the Board*, 45–47.

Hammer, M. and Champy, J. (1993). *Reengineering the Corporation: A Manifesto for Business Revolution*. New York: Harper Business.

Hammer, M. and Hershman, L. (2010). *Faster Cheaper Better: The 9 Levers for Transforming How Work Gets Done.* New York: Crown Business.

Hammer, M. and Stanton, S. (1995). *The Reengineering Revolution: The Handbook.* New York: Harper Business.

Harmon, P. (2007). *Business Process Change: A Guide for Business Managers and BPM and Six Sigma Professionals (2nd ed.).* Burlington, MA: Morgan Kaufmann Publishers.

Harvard Business Press. (2010). *Improving Business Processes (Pocket Mentor).* Boston, MA: Harvard Business Review Press.

Hassani, R., Idrissi, E. L., and Abouabdellah, A. (2018). Digital Project Management in the Era of Digital Transformation: Hybrid Method. *ICSIM2018: Proceedings of the 2018 International Conference on Software Engineering and Information Management*, 98–103.

Hossain, M. and Lassen, A. H. (2017). How Do Digital Platforms for Ideas, Technologies, and Knowledge Transfer Act as Enablers for Digital Transformation? *Information Systems & Economics eJournal.*

Johnston, G. (2012). *Business Process Re-engineering: A Simple Process Improvement Approach to Improve Business Performance (The Business Productivity Series).* Smartspeed Consulting Limited.

Khong, K. W. and Richardson, S. (2002). Examining the Effectiveness of the Critical Success Factors of Business Process Reengineering (BPR) as a Quality Management Technique in the Malaysian Banks and Financial Companies. In A. Sohal and R. Cooney (Eds.) *Sixth International Research Conference on Quality, Innovative, and Knowledge Management: Convergence in the Digital Economy* (pp. 1134–1145). Australia: Monash University.

Knights, D. and McCabe, D. (1998). 'What Happens When the Phone Goes Wild?' Staff, Stress and Spaces for Escape in a BPR Telephone Banking Work Regime. *Journal of Management Studies*, 35(2), 163–194.

Lail, J. B., Chow, L., Lam, P., Srinivasan, M., and Venkat, J. (2012). *Delivering Competitive Advantage Through BPM.* Lighthouse Point, FL: Future Strategies, Inc.

Lockamy, A. and McCormack, K. (2004). The Development of a Supply Chain Management Process Maturity Model using the Concepts of Business Process Orientation. *Supply Chain Management: An International Journal, 9*(4), 272–278.

Maedche, A., von Brocke, J., and Hevner, A. (2017). Designing the Digital Transformation: 12th International Conference, DESRIST 2017, Karlsruhe, Germany, May 30–June 1, 2017, Proceedings. New Yok: Springer.

McKinsey (2016). Supply Chain 4.0 — The Next-Generation Digital Supply Chain.

Mohapatra, S. (2012). *Business Process Reengineering: Automation Decision Points in Process Reengineering.* New York: Springer.

Ng'ang'a, R. and Kahuthu, A. N. (2013). *The Role of Managers in Business Processes Re-engineering: A HR Perspective.* Lambert Academic Publishers.

Richardson, S. (1991). *Southeast Asian Management: Cases and Concepts*. Singapore: Singapore University Press.

Richardson, S. and Khong, K. W. (2001). A comparison of business process re-engineering with other management techniques in Malaysia. In C. Nyland, W. Smith, R. Smyth, and M. Vicziany (Eds.), *Malaysian Business in the New Era* (pp. 129–147). Chichester, UK: Edward Elgar Publishing.

Rogers, D. (2016). *The Digital Transformation Playbook: Rethink Your Business for the Digital Age*. New York: Columbia Business School Publishing.

Sathananthan, S., Hoetker, P., Gamrad, D., Katterbach, D., and Myrzik, J. (2017). Realizing digital transformation through a digital business model design process. *2017 Internet of Things Business Models, Users, and Networks*.

Schallmo, D. R. A. and Williams, C. A. (2018). *Digital Transformation Now! Guiding the Successful Digitalization of Your Business Model*. New York: Springer.

Tan, A. (2007). *Business Process Reengineering in Asia: A Practical Approach (2nd ed.)*. Singapore: Pearson.

Tan, A. (2013). *Supply Chain Process Reengineering*. Prentice Hall.

West, M. (2013). *Return On Process (ROP): Getting Real Performance Results from Process Improvement*. Boca Raton, FL: CRC Press.

Yap, L. K. and Sidhu, J. S. (2001). Q&A with Chartered Bank CEO. *The Star: Business*, p. 5.

Zamzow, C. W. (2010). *Business Process — Reengineering: 7 Critical Success Factors for a Smooth Transition of Your Organizational Processes*. CreateSpace Publishing.

ABOUT THE AUTHORS

Dr. Tan is the Director for the SJTU Asia Pacific Graduate Institute based in Singapore, and associate researcher at the Massachusetts Institute of Technology Center for Transportation & Logistics. Prior to that, he was an Associate Director managing the Master program in supply chain management and logistics management in overseas universities in Dubai, Malaysia, and Singapore. His research works have been published in international journals and he is an editorial board member for various international journals.

Dr. Tan was previously a Director working in a government agency responsible for upgrading the IT capability of the manufacturing and logistics industries. This involved planning and evaluating technologies for the chemical and logistics industries. He has also provided numerous ERP and re-engineering consulting services for both discrete and process environment in Asia to streamline their supply chain while working for an IT vendor.

He is a Certified Fellow in Production and Inventory Management from APICS. He holds an MBS from the National University of Ireland and a PhD in Supply Chain Management from the Nanyang Technological University.

Sameer is a digital supply chain professional focusing on business process transformation and improvements for customers measured by useful analytics. Over the last 25 years, Sameer has acquired deep expertise in supply chain and logistics management. He has solid experience in leadership of business transformation programs and overall client engagements for ERP and supply chain initiatives.

Sameer currently helps clients enable digital business solutions from concept to proof to delivery with high customer satisfaction. He provides thought leadership for end-to-end supply chain transformation across all areas including supply chain strategy, digital supply chain planning, sourcing and procurement, inventory optimization, and outbound supply chain logistics. Leveraging deep knowledge in all these supply chain process areas, Sameer has engaged with 30 clients across manufacturing, pharmaceutical/life sciences, consumer, retail, energy, and natural resources industries.

Printed in the United States
by Baker & Taylor Publisher Services